Hands-On Edge Analytics with Azure IoT

Design and develop IoT applications with edge analytical solutions including Azure IoT Edge

Colin Dow

BIRMINGHAM - MUMBAI

Hands-On Edge Analytics with Azure IoT

Commissioning Editor: Sunith Shetty
Acquisition Editor: Devika Battike
Content Development Editor: Athikho Sapuni Rishana
Senior Editor: Roshan Kumar
Technical Editor: Manikandan Kurup
Copy Editor: Safis Editing
Project Coordinator: Aishwarya Mohan
Proofreader: Safis Editing
Indexer: Tejal Daruwale Soni
Production Designer: Aparna Bhagat

First published: May 2020

Production reference: 1200520

Published by Packt Publishing Ltd.
Livery Place
35 Livery Street
Birmingham
B3 2PB, UK.

ISBN 978-1-83882-990-2

www.packt.com

I would like to thank my wife, Constance, for her encouragement, support, and assistance; and my sons, Maximillian and Jackson, for their inspiration and optimism. I am forever grateful to them for this unique opportunity.

– Colin Dow

`Packt.com`

Subscribe to our online digital library for full access to over 7,000 books and videos, as well as industry leading tools to help you plan your personal development and advance your career. For more information, please visit our website.

Why subscribe?

- Spend less time learning and more time coding with practical eBooks and Videos from over 4,000 industry professionals

- Improve your learning with Skill Plans built especially for you

- Get a free eBook or video every month

- Fully searchable for easy access to vital information

- Copy and paste, print, and bookmark content

Did you know that Packt offers eBook versions of every book published, with PDF and ePub files available? You can upgrade to the eBook version at `www.packt.com` and as a print book customer, you are entitled to a discount on the eBook copy. Get in touch with us at `customercare@packtpub.com` for more details.

At `www.packt.com`, you can also read a collection of free technical articles, sign up for a range of free newsletters, and receive exclusive discounts and offers on Packt books and eBooks.

Contributors

About the author

Colin Dow is the author of the Packt book *Internet of Things Programming Projects*. He is also the owner and chief engineer of Sigma Rockets and Aerospace Inc, a model aerospace business. He has enjoyed working with numerous educational facilities and hobbyists in delivering product sales, presentations, and aerospace workshops over the years. He has extensive experience in creating website content, educational documentation, and instructional videos. He has been a programmer since early home computers first caught his eye. He has worked as a software developer for some of Canada's largest companies using technologies such as Python, Java, J2EE, PHP, Pearl, Ruby on Rails, Apache, SOAP web services, and many more.

About the reviewers

Parkash Karki is a principal architect, product development manager, DevOps and cloud practice head, and hardcore IoT enthusiast with years of experience in the IT field. His past experience is mainly in various Microsoft and open source technologies with a current primary focus on DevOps, automation, and the cloud. He has been working on these technologies since they were at quite an early stage. He has contributed to a few other books on IoT as a technical reviewer. He is very passionate about IoT, automation, and AI technologies and keeps on reading, blogging, and trying out different things in these areas.

Yatish Patil works with Saviant Consulting as a program manager. He has delivered enterprise IoT and analytics applications using Microsoft Azure. He has diverse industry experience in IT and has worked in a variety of domains, such as utilities, manufacturing, and engineering. He has completed the Microsoft Azure IoT certification and is the author of *Azure IoT Development Cookbook*, which focuses on the end-to-end Microsoft Azure IoT platform and pre-configured solutions. He was also the technical reviewer for the book *Microsoft Azure IaaS Essentials* and *Enterprise Internet of Things Handbook*. Yatish was among the industry speakers at India IoT Symposium 2016 and delivered a session on remote asset monitoring with Azure IoT Suite.

Packt is searching for authors like you

If you're interested in becoming an author for Packt, please visit `authors.packtpub.com` and apply today. We have worked with thousands of developers and tech professionals, just like you, to help them share their insight with the global tech community. You can make a general application, apply for a specific hot topic that we are recruiting an author for, or submit your own idea.

Table of Contents

Preface

Edge analytics has gained attention as the IoT model for connected devices and is rising in popularity. This guide will give you insights into edge analytics as a data analysis model, and why it's gaining momentum.

You'll begin with the key concepts and components used in an edge analytics app. You'll then delve into communication protocols to understand how sensors send their data to computers or microcontrollers. Next, the book will demonstrate how to design modern edge analytics apps that take advantage of the processing power of modern single-board computers and microcontrollers. Later, you'll explore Microsoft Azure IoT Edge, MicroPython, and the OpenCV visual recognition library. As you progress, you'll cover techniques for processing and AI functionality from the server side to the sensory side of IoT. You'll even explore how to design a smart doorbell system using the technologies you will have learned about. To remove vulnerabilities in the overall edge analytics architecture, you'll discover ways to overcome security and privacy challenges. Finally, you'll use tools to audit and perform real-time monitoring of incoming data and generate alerts for the infrastructure.

By the end of this book, you'll have learned how to use edge analytics programming techniques and implement automated analytical computations.

Who this book is for

If you are a data analyst, data architect, or data scientist who is interested in learning and practicing advanced automated analytical computations, then this book is for you. You will also find this book useful if you're looking to learn edge analytics from scratch. Basic knowledge of data analytics concepts is assumed and required to get the most out of this book.

What this book covers

Chapter 1, *Introduction to Edge Analytics*, outlines how everything old is new again! The rise of the personal computer in the 1980s and 1990s led to a revolution in computing. Instead of so-called *dumb* terminals connected to a large computer, many computers were connected in a network spreading the processing power around. Edge analytics is like the personal computer revolution but for **Internet-of-Things** (**IoT**) devices. We will start this chapter by comparing edge analytics to the computer revolution before we discuss the advantages of using edge analytics in an IoT application. We will both look at the basic edge analytics architecture and introduce the Microsoft Azure IoT Edge platform.

Chapter 2, *How Does IoT Edge Analytics Work?*, discusses the components used in an edge analytics application and how they fit together. Now that we understand what edge analytics is, let's turn our attention to how it works. In this chapter, we will conclude by looking at real-world edge analytics applications.

Chapter 3, *Communications Protocols Used in Edge Analytics*, outlines how one part of an IoT or edge analytics application is the connection to the internet. The other part is the connection from our edge device to the sensors. In this chapter, we will explore ways by which we can connect our edge device to the internet. We will look at some of the long-distance technologies, as well as the familiar Wi-Fi protocol. In our exploration of Wi-Fi, we will gain an understanding as to the radio frequency spectrum and where different communication protocols fit into this spectrum. We will also take a look at Bluetooth and consider how we may use it in our applications.

Chapter 4, *Working with Microsoft Azure IoT Hub*, is the beginning of our work with Azure IoT services using Microsoft Azure, after Chapter 1, *Introduction to Edge Analytics*, where we touched on Azure IoT Edge and Azure IoT. The lessons learned from this will provide a good basis for using the Raspberry Pi with Azure IoT Edge.

Chapter 5, *Using the Raspberry Pi with Azure IoT Edge*, builds on what we covered in Chapter 4, *Working with Microsoft Azure IoT Hub*, where we learned a bit about Microsoft Azure and the IoT Hub in Azure. This background is essential to understanding Azure IoT Edge. In this chapter, we will learn how to install Azure IoT Edge on the Raspberry Pi and read data from it using the Microsoft Device Explorer.

Chapter 6, *Using MicroPython for Edge Analytics*, covers MicroPython as a subset of Python 3. MicroPython was developed as a programming language for microcontrollers. With microcontrollers getting more and more powerful, learning MicroPython is becoming more essential. Imagine having the ability to take your Python knowledge and apply it to the physical world. Imagine building lightweight, energy-efficient, and powerful edge analytics applications with all the advantages of using the Python programming language. With MicroPython, you can.

Chapter 7, *Machine Learning and Edge Analytics*, considers one of the most exciting fields in the realm of technology today—machine learning. As this technology matures and gets into the hands of more and more people, exciting new applications are created, such as a tool for detecting respiratory diseases based on audio analysis of breathing patterns.

By combining edge analytics with machine learning, the capabilities on the sensory side are vast. This, combined with the ever-increasing power of microcontrollers and single-board computers such as the Raspberry Pi, means that the future looks very bright indeed for edge analytics and machine learning.

In this chapter, we will explore the advantages of machine learning at the edge with a Raspberry Pi as we write a program to distinguish between the face of a person and the face of a dog. We will then jump into the exciting new world of **Artificial Intelligence of Things (AIoT)** as we take a small microcontroller and turn it into a QR code decoder tool.

Chapter 8, *Designing a Smart Doorbell with Visual Recognition*, remembers how years ago, the only way to recognize who was knocking at your door without being too obvious was to peer through a little peephole near the top of the door. Observant visitors would notice the light disappear from the peephole once a face was pressed up against it on the other side. So, in other words, we really weren't fooling anyone into thinking we weren't home if we decided that the visitor was not worthy of us opening the door. Times have certainly changed. We have the technology now to filter unwanted visitors for us without being detected. Using a camera and vision recognition algorithms on the sensory side, we will design an edge analytics application that alerts us to who is at the door.

Chapter 9, *Security and Privacy in an Edge Analytics World*, covers how, when deploying an application to the internet, the risks posed by cybercriminals should be taken very seriously. Internet-enabled devices including edge computers are prone to cyber-attacks where they may be used to shut down websites or cause havoc on the internet, not to mention the destruction of our networked applications. In this chapter, we will cover security and in turn, privacy, when it comes to our edge analytics applications.

Chapter 10, *What Next?*, examines where we are at the end of our edge analytics journey. I hope you enjoyed the ride. *Tell them what you are going to tell them, tell them, and then tell them what you just told them*—those are the great words of wisdom given to me by the more seasoned speakers at my Toastmasters club. In this chapter, we will recap what we have learned and then look ahead to the future of edge analytics.

To get the most out of this book

To get the most out of this book, having the following will be beneficial:

- In Chapter 2, *How Does IoT Edge Analytics Work?*, we will use an ESP8266 with an RGB LED to create a weather forecasting application.
- In Chapter 5, *Using the Raspberry Pi with Azure IoT Edge*, we will install Azure IoT Edge onto a Raspberry Pi 3B+. Although there is a newer version of the Raspberry Pi (the Raspberry Pi 4), the Raspberry Pi 3B+ will be needed in order to install an older version of the Raspbian operating system.
- A computer with Windows installed will be needed to run the Microsoft Device Explorer tool that we will use in Chapter 4, *Working with Microsoft Azure IoT Hub*, and Chapter 5, *Using the Raspberry Pi with Azure IoT Edge*.
- The purchase of an ESP32 with LoRa and the Pycom LoPy/LoPy 4 will assist in Chapter 6, *Using MicroPython for Edge Analytics*, as we cover MicroPython and microcontrollers.
- A webcam will be used in Chapter 8, *Designing a Smart Doorbell with Visual Recognition*, as we build our smart doorbell application.

Software/hardware covered in the book	OS requirements
Raspberry Pi 3B+	Raspbian Stretch
Pycom LoPy / LoPy 4	Latest MicroPython firmware from Pycom
ESP32 with LoRa	Latest version of MicroPython
ESP8266	Default firmware
RGB LED	
DHT11 temperature sensor	
PC	Windows 10 and Node-RED

If you are using the digital version of this book, we advise you to type the code yourself or access the code via the GitHub repository (link available in the next section). Doing so will help you avoid any potential errors related to the copying and pasting of code.

Download the example code files

You can download the example code files for this book from your account at www.packt.com. If you purchased this book elsewhere, you can visit www.packtpub.com/support and register to have the files emailed directly to you.

You can download the code files by following these steps:

1. Log in or register at www.packt.com.
2. Select the **Support** tab.
3. Click on **Code Downloads**.
4. Enter the name of the book in the **Search** box and follow the onscreen instructions.

Once the file is downloaded, please make sure that you unzip or extract the folder using the latest version of:

- WinRAR/7-Zip for Windows
- Zipeg/iZip/UnRarX for Mac
- 7-Zip/PeaZip for Linux

The code bundle for the book is also hosted on GitHub at https://github.com/PacktPublishing/Hands-On-Edge-Analytics-with-Azure-IoT. In case there's an update to the code, it will be updated on the existing GitHub repository.

We also have other code bundles from our rich catalog of books and videos available at https://github.com/PacktPublishing/. Check them out!

Download the color images

We also provide a PDF file that has color images of the screenshots/diagrams used in this book. You can download it here: https://static.packt-cdn.com/downloads/9781838829902_ColorImages.pdf.

Conventions used

There are a number of text conventions used throughout this book.

`CodeInText`: Indicates code words in text, database table names, folder names, filenames, file extensions, pathnames, dummy URLs, user input, and Twitter handles. Here is an example: "The `LoRaMessage` class is used to send LoRa messages to the gateway device."

A block of code is set as follows:

```
import pycom
import time

pycom.heartbeat(False)

while True:
    pycom.rgbled(0xFF0000) # Red
    time.sleep(1)
    pycom.rgbled(0x00FF00) # Green
    time.sleep(1)
    pycom.rgbled(0x0000FF) # Blue
    time.sle
```

Any command-line input or output is written as follows:

```
$ sudo apt-get update
$ sudo apt-get install moby-engine
```

Bold: Indicates a new term, an important word, or words that you see onscreen. For example, words in menus or dialog boxes appear in the text like this. Here is an example: "Review your instance before clicking on the green **+ Create New Instance button**."

Warnings or important notes appear like this.

Tips and tricks appear like this.

Get in touch

Feedback from our readers is always welcome.

General feedback: If you have questions about any aspect of this book, mention the book title in the subject of your message and email us at customercare@packtpub.com.

Errata: Although we have taken every care to ensure the accuracy of our content, mistakes do happen. If you have found a mistake in this book, we would be grateful if you would report this to us. Please visit www.packtpub.com/support/errata, selecting your book, clicking on the Errata Submission Form link, and entering the details.

Piracy: If you come across any illegal copies of our works in any form on the Internet, we would be grateful if you would provide us with the location address or website name. Please contact us at copyright@packt.com with a link to the material.

If you are interested in becoming an author: If there is a topic that you have expertise in and you are interested in either writing or contributing to a book, please visit authors.packtpub.com.

Reviews

Please leave a review. Once you have read and used this book, why not leave a review on the site that you purchased it from? Potential readers can then see and use your unbiased opinion to make purchase decisions, we at Packt can understand what you think about our products, and our authors can see your feedback on their book. Thank you!

For more information about Packt, please visit packt.com.

Section 1: Getting Started with Edge Analytics

What is edge analytics? How does understanding edge analytics help me as a developer? If such questions come to mind for you, then the following chapters will assist you in understanding this exciting new technology.

This section comprises the following chapters:

- Chapter 1, *Introduction to Edge Analytics*
- Chapter 2, *How Does IoT Edge Analytics Work?*
- Chapter 3, *Communication Protocols Used in Edge Analytics*

Introduction to Edge Analytics

Everything old is new again! The rise of the **personal computer** (**PC**) in the 1980s and 1990s led to a revolution in computing. Instead of so-called *dumb* terminals connected to a large computer, many computers were connected in a network, spreading the processing power around. Edge analytics is like the personal computer revolution, but for **IoT** (**Internet of Things**) devices. We will start this chapter by comparing edge analytics to the computer revolution before we discuss the advantages of using edge analytics in an IoT application. We will look at the basic edge analytics architecture, as well as introduce the Microsoft Azure IoT Edge platform.

This chapter will cover the following topics:

- What is edge analytics?
- Applying and comparing architectures
- Key benefits of edge analytics
- Edge analytics architectures
- Using edge analytics in the real world

What is edge analytics?

In order to build on the statement that edge analytics is *like the personal computer revolution, but for IoT devices,* let's take a technological step back and look at the way application computing used to be done. We'll start by taking a customary look at early computers.

Early computers

Operators of early digital computers accessed the computer through paper punch cards, paper tape readout, blinking lights, and teletype machines adapted for computer use. By the mid-1960s, **CRT** (known as **cathode ray tube**) displays were used as displays in place of paper, allowing for better flexibility. CRT displays were the technology of television sets at the time. By the mid-1970s, *dumb* terminals using CRT screens and typewriter keyboards were the standards in interacting with a computer.

 In 1943, Thomas Watson, the president of IBM, famously predicted that there was a world market for a *possible five computers*. In hindsight, this prediction was incredibly wrong. Watson could not have possibly envisioned the technological advancements in computing since the time of his prediction. It is estimated that there are over 2 billion personal computers in use today.

The following diagram shows a mid-1970s computer (called a **mainframe**) and a dumb terminal. A system such as this would be used by operators for applications such as booking hotel rooms and checking inventory levels:

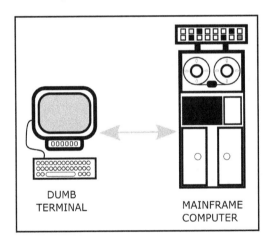

In this arrangement, the dumb terminal was used only for displaying and entering data. The processing was done by the mainframe computer. Access to the mainframe was controlled by system administrators. The dumb terminal and mainframe would dominate the 1970s; however, a growing interest in bringing computing power to hobbyists and would-be programmers was starting to brew. This period of time would prove to be the dawning of the personal computer era.

The rise of the personal computer

By the mid-1970s, personal computers were starting to make their way into the market place in a meaningful way. The term **personal computer** was used when the Altair 8800 was introduced in December 1974. The first Apple computer was released 2 years later. By the mid-1980s, there were many personal computers for technologists and hobbyists to choose from, including the PC from IBM, the Commodore 64, and the Atari Amiga. The following image shows the Sinclair ZX81 computer from 1982. Despite its limited 1 KB memory, this very ZX81 would start yours truly on the path to becoming a computer nerd:

Users of early personal computers were free from depending on system administrators for mainframe access. The personal computer spawned a new generation of programmers who now had more control over their devices than ever before. Advancements in microelectronics created increasingly better personal computers and the prices continued to fall. Early applications for personal computers included word processing, spreadsheet programs, and—of course—games.

Peer-to-peer networks

It wasn't long before personal computers were connected together in networks, where their collective power could be utilized. Computations performed by powerful mainframes could now be spread across many personal computers in a method known as **distributed computing**.

With the arrival of the internet on April 30, 1993, personal computers were able to connect to other personal computers anywhere in the world. Early **peer-to-peer** (**P2P**) networks allowed users to share files with each other over the entire world. The following diagram shows such a network:

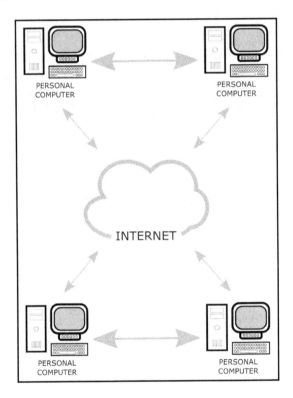

 SETI@home is a distributed computing project designed to analyze radio signals in order to look for signs of extraterrestrial intelligence. SETI@home depends on volunteers who donate their internet-connected computer's downtime to the distributed network. With this architecture, SETI@home is the largest supercomputer in the world.

P2P networks became notorious for digital piracy. P2P applications such as Napster allowed users to share songs over the internet with others, bypassing copyright laws. Despite this, P2P networks continued to flourish. Blockchain, the technology behind Bitcoin, operates on a P2P network of computers that each hold an identical copy of a ledger of transactions.

Cloud computing

As applications became more resource-intensive, more and more computing power was needed. Server rooms with powerful PCs popped up in businesses all over the world, with staff hired to maintain these servers. It soon became obvious that it was far more cost-effective to shift server resources outside of the company to the internet, or what is commonly referred to as the cloud. Thus, cloud computing became a reality.

So, what exactly is cloud computing? Why should an organization use cloud computing? The following high-level diagram shows what cloud computing looks like:

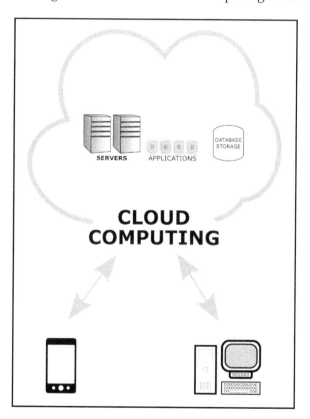

As you can see, the servers, applications, and database storage exist in the cloud. These resources are accessed by the client's device (in this case, cell phone or PC) through the internet. Companies that push their resources to the cloud do not have to carry the expense or worry of running a server room. They pay only for the resources they use, thus they reduce their expenses.

One of the first cloud services offered was the Amazon **Elastic Compute Cloud** (or **EC2**). EC2 is central to Amazon's cloud service offering, **Amazon Web Services** (**AWS**), and was released to the public in 2006. Other cloud service providers include the **Google Cloud Platform** (**GCP**) and Microsoft Azure.

Edge computing

Edge computing is a form of distributed computing whereby resources are copied from a remote location to a local one. See the following diagram:

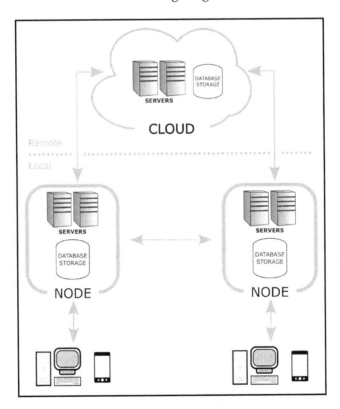

As you can see, there is a central cloud network of servers and database storage, and nodes of servers and databases connected to the central cloud. The cloud-based network exists in a remote location. This could be on the other side of the world, for example. The nodes are located locally, perhaps in the same physical building as the computers that will access them.

 Edge computing will be used in the upcoming 5G cellular data standard, as locally distributed nodes will provide access to the network with lightning speeds. With the rapid rise in the number of IoT devices connected, 5G will allow for sensors to transmit data with a small amount of latency.

Despite improvements to network technology, having nodes close to the location where they are needed is a methodology worth the extra cost due to the following three factors:

- Privacy
- Latency
- Reliability

We will go into more detail on these three factors in the upcoming section *Edge analytics*.

Now that we have an understanding of the various options for computing resources, let's take a look at IoT applications.

Early IoT applications

Early IoT applications were much like the old mainframe and dumb terminal computing architecture. In these applications, remote sensors send basic data to a computer through an internet- (cloud-) connected microcontroller.

The following diagram shows an IoT application using a temperature sensor and an ESP8266 internet-connected microcontroller:

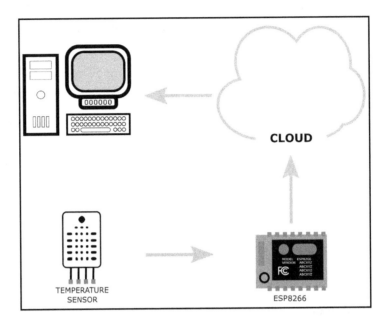

As you can see, the *thing* in the IoT application does nothing more than read the temperature. The ESP8266 microcontroller passes the sensory data along to a web service using the internet (cloud). The processing of sensory data is done by a computer or a series of computers on the other side of the cloud.

Edge analytics

Edge analytics removes some of the processing burden from the internet-connected computer. Instead of just sending sensory information, as is the case in the early IoT solutions, an edge analytics architecture processes the data at the source (*the edge*), thereby limiting the amount of data sent back. Edge analytics takes its name from edge computing. An edge analytics application benefits from resources close to where they are needed, just as other edge computing applications do. The following diagram shows a basic edge analytics application:

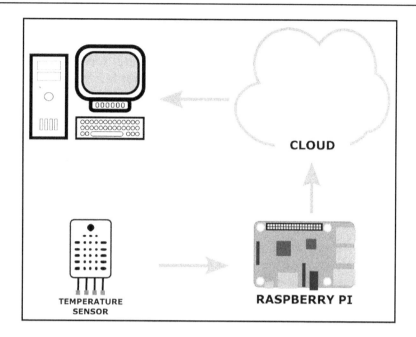

As you can see in the diagram, a Raspberry Pi is used in place of a microcontroller to communicate with the temperature sensor. Being a single-board computer, the Raspberry Pi is far more powerful than a microcontroller such as the ESP8266. Although the preceding diagram only shows one sensor connected to the Raspberry Pi, it could show many more. The Raspberry Pi contains an entire operating system and built-in programming environments that make it relatively easy to access sensory information and process it.

At the time of writing this book, the Raspberry Pi 4 Model B was a few months old. The Raspberry Pi 4 Model B features dual 4K monitor support, a faster processor, up to 4 GB of **random-access memory** (**RAM**), and two **Universal Serial Bus** (**USB**) 3 ports. This new release has taken the Raspberry Pi from an embedded computer for maker projects into the domain of desktop computing.

While our analogy of edge analytics being similar to the personal computer revolution may not be perfect, it is possible to see the correlation between the two concepts. The history of computing seems to always go back and forth between central processing control and distributed processing or edge processing. Edge analytics for IoT falls into the latter category.

Applying and comparing architectures

What are the advantages of using an edge analytics architecture over a standard IoT architecture? Why go with a more expensive and complicated edge analytics solution over a basic IoT one? To answer these questions, let's outline a potential business model and apply both architectures to it.

Let's suppose you are an entrepreneur and you introduce the world to an exciting new soft drink, Edge Cola. Business is growing swiftly and you roll out your new soft drink with high-tech vending machines. You've heard of IoT and wonder how it could work with your vending machines.

Would a standard IoT architecture work for your business, or should you look into edge analytics?

The standard IoT solution

The following diagram shows the standard IoT solution that you would take for your high-tech vending machines:

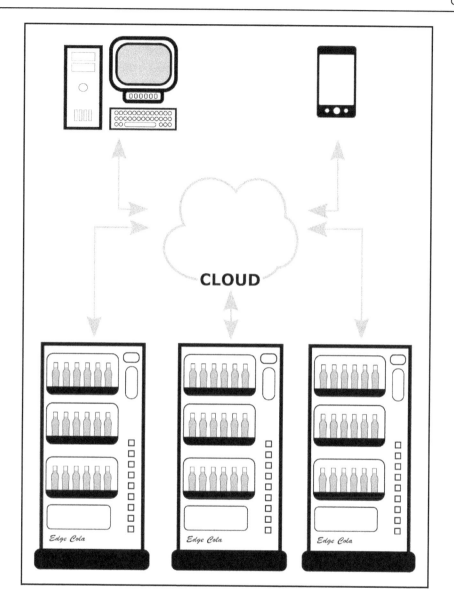

Arguably the world's first IoT device was a network-connected altered Coke machine developed by graduate students at **Carnegie Mellon University** (**CMU**) in the early 1980s. The students from this school in Pittsburgh, Pennsylvania found their Coke machine was located inconveniently far away. Many times, a trip down to the machine resulted in finding a machine void of Coke, or worse, Cokes that were too warm. The application they developed not only told them if a Coke was available but also whether or not the Cokes in the machine were cold.

As you can see from the preceding diagram, each vending machine sends sensory information to the cloud, where an IoT dashboard arranges it in a clean interface. You are able to view your IoT dashboard on any device you choose, whether that be a PC, tablet, or cell phone.

Business is going really well. You can't keep up with demand. You are rolling out new vending machines as fast as you can. As a result, your dashboard is constantly having to keep up with more and more data coming in. Your IoT software vendor can't keep up with the increasing demand on its systems. Your sensory data is competing with the data coming in from the vendor's other customers. Your dashboard is no longer accurate. This is due to the inherent flaws of using the cloud to process simple telemetry data. It simply takes too long and is too inefficient to send sensory data up to the cloud. As well, your cellular data costs are too high, as each vending machine is constantly sending sensory data to the cloud even if the data has not changed.

How can you improve your architecture? Using an edge analytics approach could be the answer to these issues.

Edge analytics-based IoT solution

In our standard IoT architecture, it is obvious that the bottleneck in the system is the constant flow of sensory data. This flow overwhelms your IoT dashboard vendor and results in high cellular data charges. Most of the time, the sensory data is unchanged from one transmission to the other. Your architecture is inefficient.

A smarter approach would be to use edge analytics and push off some of the processing to the *edge*. The following diagram shows the new and improved architecture using edge analytics:

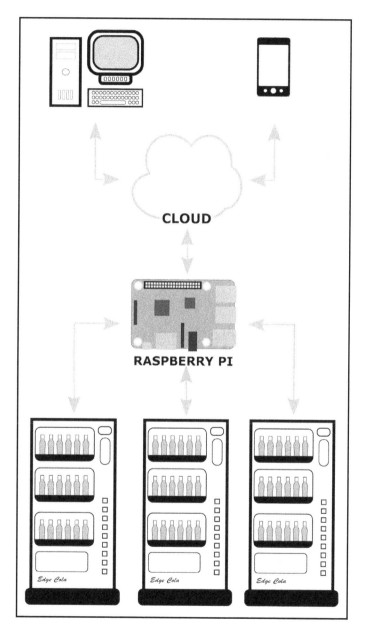

As you can see, the vending machines are now connected to a gateway (in this case, a Raspberry Pi). Sensory data is read by the gateway instead of being sent directly into the cloud. The gateway will only send sensory data when there has been a change. This alleviates the IoT dashboard from constantly reading sensory data. Cellular data usage is also reduced.

We could build intelligence into our gateway whereby data is analyzed and messages could be sent back to the IoT dashboard. For example, if machine A seems to be constantly out of stock on Tuesdays before 4 p.m., a reminder message to refill this machine could appear on the IoT dashboard at the appropriate time.

Another intelligent function could be to compare sales from side-by-side machines with different refrigerated temperatures. Over time, one machine may dispense far more than the other, giving you an idea as to the optimal temperature for your product.

Taking the edge analytics approach, you alleviate the strain of constant network traffic and cloud processing in the system. Costs are reduced, and the system is far more efficient and up to date.

Now that we have a rudimentary understanding of edge analytics, let's take a look at the key concepts and benefits.

Key benefits of edge analytics

As we have seen in the previous section, implementing edge analytics into our IoT design has advantages that outweigh the costs and complexity. However, before we can build an edge analytics system, we need to know what the key benefits are.

The following is a list of those benefits (note that these are the same key benefits as described in the *Edge computing* section):

- Privacy
- Latency
- Reliability

Let's take a look at an example. In the following diagram, we have designed an advanced security application using an edge analytics architecture. As you can see, we have a Raspberry Pi connected to a webcam, automated door, and a light sensor:

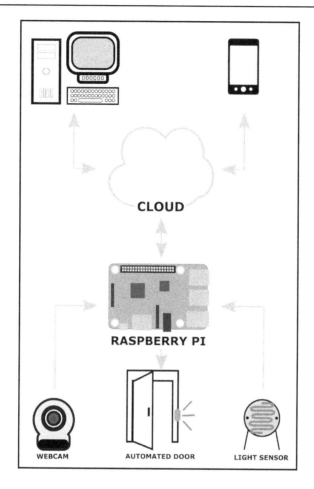

CLOUD

RASPBERRY PI

WEBCAM   AUTOMATED DOOR   LIGHT SENSOR

Our advanced security application uses the webcam and Raspberry Pi to recognize a visitor trying to gain access to the building. Based on the match of our visitor with a repository of known visitors, our advanced security application would open certain doors. The light sensor would let our application know if lights are on in the rooms that the recognized visitor has access to, and turn them on prior to this person entering them.

Our design allows IoT data to be sent from the Raspberry Pi to the cloud. We could use this data in a remote dashboard app. A remote security agent could provide an override if, for example, our application could not make a match of a legitimate visitor.

Let's now expand on the key benefits, as these relate to our advanced security application.

Privacy

For some organizations, having company data stored in the cloud is not permitted. With our advanced security application, the webcam is used to take pictures and recognize people. This information is personal, and it would be inappropriate to store it on a server outside of the organization. Thus, sending image data to the cloud for processing would not be possible.

Our advanced security application benefits by having an edge analytics architecture in that the privacy of the information—in this case, personal photos—is stored on the premises.

Latency

In our design, we can easily see how latency—or the time taken to do something—can play a part. The image recognition algorithm would have to work very quickly. Sending the task of processing images to the cloud would take too much time, which would make our system inefficient.

The reduced latency benefit of an edge analytics architecture results in a system that is quick to respond. The wait time for visitors at the door is much shorter than if processing information were pushed off to the internet.

Reliability

As we have control of our internal systems, we can react accordingly in the event of system failure. Systems outside of our organization may experience downtimes or periods where they may not be able to keep up with processing requests. Our advanced security application is more reliable as we are not at the mercy of computer systems outside of our control. In addition to this, if our application were deployed at a remote location, access to a reliable internet connection may be an issue to deal with.

Let's take a look at some edge analytics architectures to see how we may utilize these key concepts.

Edge analytics architectures

As with any application we design, when the time comes to design an edge analytics application, it is good to explore the options available. We will start off this section looking at a basic edge analytics architecture—one that does not involve using a vendor-specific solution. We will then turn our attention to the Microsoft Azure IoT platform and Microsoft Azure IoT Edge.

Basic edge analytics architecture

By basic edge analytics architecture, I am referring to an environment where the platform is made up of just the core physical components—a system where a standard operating system with custom code is used in place of a platform such as Microsoft Azure IoT. Let's face it—there are times when a simple solution is required and the costs of a vendor-specific platform cannot be justified.

A basic edge analytics application consists of three major components. They are as follows:

- Sensors and actuators
- Edge computers
- Cloud-based dashboards

We can see how these components are connected together in the following diagram:

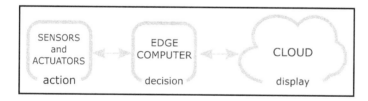

As we can see in the preceding diagram, our sensors and actuators are responsible for the action in our edge analytics application. These actions could be such things as taking the temperature using a DHT11 sensor or opening up a door, as is the case for actuators.

The decisions made in our edge analytics happen with the edge computer. The edge computer could be as simple as a microcontroller or as powerful as a quad-core desktop computer. What makes the computer an edge computer is its close proximity to the sensor and actuators.

The cloud used in our edge analytics application is responsible for dashboards and messaging to our devices. We may also use the cloud to create a control interface that may override decisions made by the edge computer.

We will be looking at the physical components used in this architecture in Chapter 2, *How Does IoT Edge Analytics Work?*

Azure IoT Edge-based edge analytics architecture

For more advanced edge analytics applications, such as those requiring a vendor-specific machine learning algorithm, then a platform such as Microsoft Azure IoT Edge is desired. What exactly is Microsoft Azure IoT Edge, and why would we use it? Before we can answer these questions, let's take a look at Microsoft Azure IoT.

Understanding Microsoft Azure IoT

Microsoft Azure IoT is a collection of Microsoft Azure cloud services used to build IoT applications. Microsoft Azure IoT applications are built using physical sensors and the Azure web portal. Access to the web portal is controlled through an Azure account. The following diagram shows a typical IoT application using Microsoft Azure IoT:

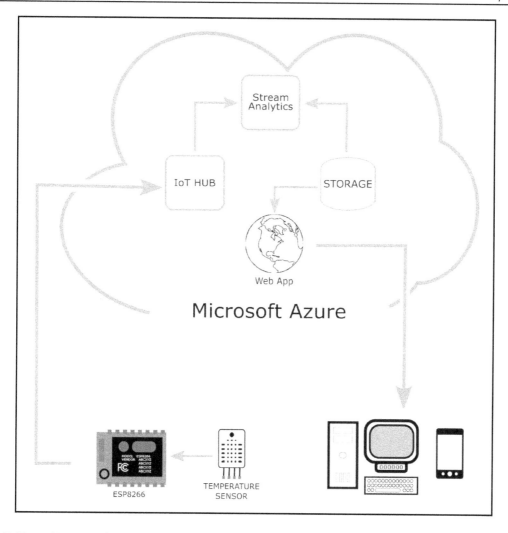

The IoT application shown in the preceding diagram is similar to the ones we've designed earlier in this chapter. It features a temperature sensor hooked up to an ESP8266 microcontroller. Data from the ESP8266 microcontroller is sent to the Azure cloud service. Using the Azure portal, we would configure the IoT Hub, Stream Analytics, Storage, and Web App components.

Using the Microsoft Azure IoT platform instead of building our own platform, we are able to utilize pre-written code, as well as have an infrastructure already set up. We do not need to buy and set up our own servers or configure a hosted web server. This saves us time as well as money, as we only pay for what we need. We will cover these concepts in more detail in `Chapter 4`, *Working with Microsoft Azure IoT Hub*.

Now that we have an understanding of Microsoft Azure IoT, let's take a look at Azure IoT Edge.

Understanding Microsoft Azure IoT Edge

So, what exactly is Microsoft Azure IoT Edge? How does it differ from the other edge analytics applications we have discussed up till now? We can understand Azure IoT Edge a little bit better if we view Azure IoT Hub as if it were a typical remote server, and the installation of Azure IoT Edge on a physical edge device as if it were an edge computing platform. More precisely, though, Azure IoT Edge is a form of distributed computing whereby Azure modules are copied to the physical edge device, as illustrated in the following diagram:

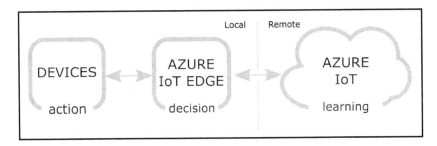

In the preceding diagram, we can see that Azure IoT is remote-based and the Azure IoT Edge installation is a locally based node. The devices (which are similar to the sensors and actuators mentioned in the previous section) are locally based as well and take advantage of having a node version of Azure IoT in the form of Azure IoT Edge. So, in other words, Azure IoT Edge brings the advantages of edge computing to Azure-based IoT applications. We will revisit and go into more detail about this diagram in `Chapter 2`, *How Does IoT Edge Analytics work?*.

Using edge analytics in the real world

As with any technology, it is easy to get excited by its possibilities. However, before dedicating time to learning a new technology, the real-world usages of it may be called into question. Is anyone or any organization using this technology today?

For the American company Mars Drinks, keeping their vending machines fully stocked is very important for retaining customers. Mars Drinks rolled out a Microsoft Azure IoT Edge solution for just that purpose.

Route optimization directs service experts in their day-to-day operations restocking the machines. Using data analyzed from the vending machines, a service route may be planned or modified based on individual machine inventory. This makes the day-to-day task of the service experts in charge of refilling the machines more efficient.

Historical weather information collected by the Azure platform helps Mars Drinks in designing their menu options. Menu options may be modified to reflect consumption patterns, based on the analysis.

Azure IoT Edge and related cloud services have helped Mars Drinks become a data-driven company focused on the needs of the consumer. Azure IoT and Azure IoT Edge have led to improved operational efficiency, new business insights, and support for global expansion in a rapidly changing world.

Summary

In this chapter, we began by touching briefly on the various computing platforms. We described how the mainframe computer with accompanying dumb terminals was superseded in part by the rise of connected personal computers, and how this was similar to the difference between an IoT application and an edge analytics one. We discussed how edge analytics is really just an edge computing paradigm.

We then looked at the advantages of using edge analytics over a traditional IoT application. We described a scenario where a vending machine uses a standard IoT solution, and the challenges this type of approach has.

We also started looking at the Microsoft Azure IoT offering. We discussed Microsoft Azure IoT Edge and how this relates to Azure IoT.

We concluded the chapter with a cursory look at a real-world example of the Microsoft Azure IoT Edge platform. In the next chapter, we will be expanding on the concepts learned in this chapter, and start to dig deeper into the actual components that make up an edge analytics application.

Questions

Having learned the lessons in this chapter, try answering the following questions on your own:

1. True/False. Edge analytics is about processing data at the sensory level.
2. True/False. The *first* IoT device was a vending machine built by graduate students at CMU.
3. How many computers did Thomas Watson say the world would ever need?
4. What are the three key benefits of edge analytics to be understood?
5. True/False. The automated door used in our security application may be controlled anywhere in the world.
6. What are the advantages of using edge computing?
7. True/False. Azure IoT Edge and edge computing share the same advantages.
8. What were some of the uses of early P2P networks?
9. True/False. Microsoft Azure IoT is a collection of Azure services used to build IoT applications.
10. True/False. Route optimization was one of the benefits to Mars Drinks of using Azure IoT.

How Does IoT Edge Analytics Work? ²

Now that we understand what edge analytics is, let's turn our attention to how it works. In this chapter, we will discuss the components used in an edge analytics application and how they fit together. By the end of this chapter, we should not only have a better understanding of edge analytics, but an understanding that is rooted in the practical use of it.

We will conclude this chapter by looking at real-world edge analytics applications.

This chapter will cover the following topics:

- What are the components used in an edge analytics application?
- How do the components fit together?
- More examples of real-world edge analytics applications.

What are the components used in an edge analytics application?

As we have learned in the previous chapter, to build an edge analytics application, there are certain components that we must use. In the following sections, we will expand on basic components before taking a look at components specific to Microsoft Azure.

Basic edge analytics components

If we were to build a simple edge analytics application from scratch, we would require sensors for measurement, a microcontroller or computer for processing this information, a connection to the internet for sending this information, and of course a cloud service of some sort to acquire and display the information. In this section, we will discuss what could be considered basic edge analytics applications.

Sensors

Without sensors, our edge analytics application would not be able to measure the world around us. Some of the more popular sensors measure temperature, humidity, and motion. Others measure parameters such as fluid flow control through a pipe or the density of the air.

The following sections discuss some of the sensors we may use in our edge analytics applications.

DHT11 temperature and humidity sensor

The DHT11 temperature and humidity sensor is a low-cost device used in IoT applications. There are API libraries for this sensor from such sources as Adafruit Industries, which makes it easy to implement the DHT11 into an IoT or edge analytics application.

The following is a Fritzing diagram of how a DHT11 temperature and humidity sensor could be hooked up in an edge analytics application:

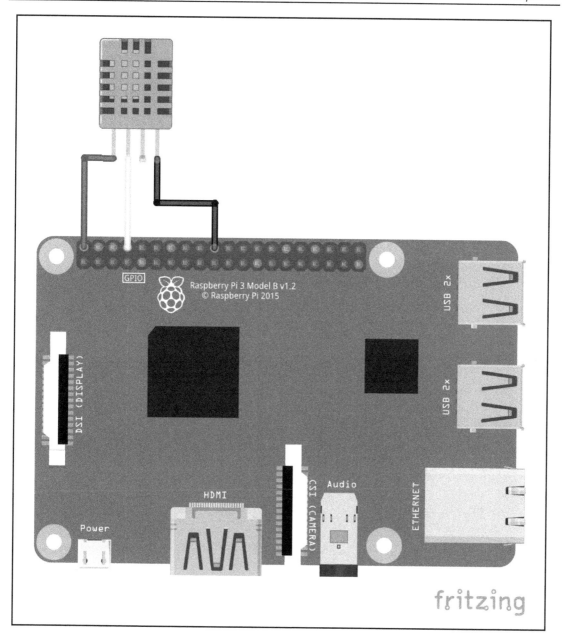

First released on June 3, 2016, Fritzing is an open source software program used to design electronic circuits. It's free to use and is available for macOS, Windows, and Linux. It features an easy-to-use GUI interface with an extensive library of electronic components to include in the user's designs. Outside components may be easily added as well. To find out more about this amazing program, go to www.fritzing.org.

The following is a code example using the DHT11 and the Python programming language. The code was written for the Raspberry Pi and is taken from my first book, *Internet of Things Programming Projects* (Packt Publishing). This code uses the Adafruit DHT library to measure temperature and humidity and send this information to a cloud-based dashboard using the MQTT protocol:

```python
from time import sleep
import Adafruit_DHT
import paho.mqtt.client as mqtt
import json

host = 'demo.thingsboard.io'
access_token = '<<access token>>'
dht_sensor = Adafruit_DHT.DHT11
pin = 19

sensor_data = {'temperature': 0, 'humidity': 0}

client = mqtt.Client()
client.username_pw_set(access_token)

while True:
    humidity, temperature = Adafruit_DHT
                        .read_retry(dht_sensor, pin)

    print(u"Temperature: {:g}\u00b0C, Humidity{:g}%".format(temperature, \
            humidity))

    sensor_data['temperature'] = temperature
    sensor_data['humidity'] = humidity
    client.connect(host, 1883, 20)
    client.publish('v1/devices/me/telemetry',
                json.dumps(sensor_data), 1)
    client.disconnect()
    sleep(10)
```

The preceding code was written for an IoT application, not an edge analytics one. However, it does point out how easily information from a sensor may be read and utilized.

Soil moisture sensor

If you wanted to build an automated smart garden system, having a soil moisture sensor is required. The name of this sensor is pretty self-explanatory: it measures the moisture level in the soil. The following is a photograph of a soil moisture sensor:

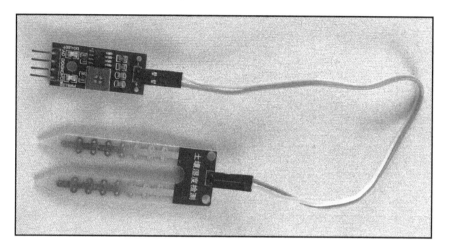

As you can see in the photograph, the sensor is made up of two parts. The bottom piece is the part that is actually inserted into the soil. It connects to the other piece, the controller, via a wire. The four pins in the controller are as follows:

- **VCC**: Used to provide power to the sensor
- **GND**: For ground
- **D0**: For digital output (either high or low) from the sensor
- **A0:** For analog output from the sensor

The following diagram is an example of an edge analytics application using a soil moisture sensor. As you can see, one end of the moisture sensor is inserted into the soil of our plant pot. The other end of the sensor is connected to our Raspberry Pi computer. This allows our Raspberry Pi access to the soil moisture data:

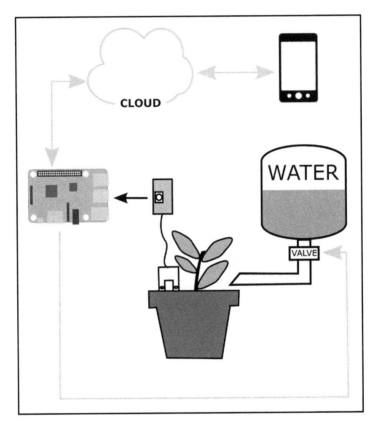

Our Raspberry Pi uses this data to determine when to open the valve and add more water to our plant. Our Raspberry Pi also sends data to the cloud to which we would connect our computer or device. This data may be as simple as the soil level, or it may be modified in some way by our Raspberry Pi before it is sent to the cloud.

It is the logic programmed into our Raspberry Pi that makes our application an edge analytics one as opposed to a standard IoT application that would just send the reading.

Laser sensor

You may have seen those movies where the spy is trying to break into a high-security compound for some reason or another. There are usually laser beams spread out in places that are impossible to avoid.

Laser sensors are an important part of security applications. The following is a photograph of a laser sensor:

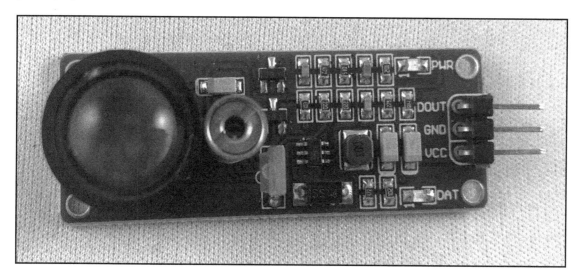

There are three pins in the preceding laser sensor. They are as follows:

- **VCC**: For power
- **GND**: For ground
- **DOUT:** For digital output signal

The following is a simple alarm system using a laser sensor. As with our smart garden, the processing logic programmed onto the Raspberry Pi makes this an edge analytics application:

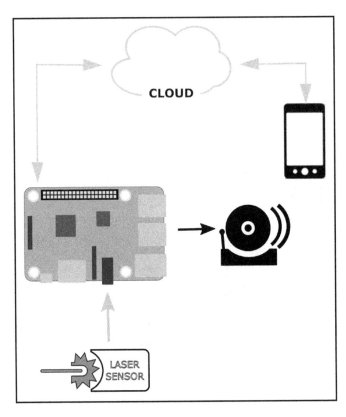

 Light Amplification by Stimulated Emission of Radiation, or **LASER** for short, had its origins in the theoretical foundations of Albert Einstein in 1917. The year 2020 marks the 60th anniversary of the laser as Theodore H. Maiman of Hughes Research Laboratories invented the first one in 1960. Early lasers were used in medical procedures. Today, we may find lasers in everything from DVD players to laser pointers and **Light Detection and Ranging (LiDAR)**.

By having the processing done on the Raspberry Pi, we can limit or modify the data sent to the cloud. For example, the logic may be programmed to send text messages only to certain people at night or on weekends.

Microcontrollers and computers

To build an edge analytics application, an edge device is required. This edge device is either a microcontroller or a computer of some sort. The edge device is physically located close to the sensors it is connected to. In the following sections, we will look at various devices that may be used as edge devices.

The ESP8266

The ESP8266 chip first came to critical attention in 2014 with the ESP-01 module. The low cost of the ESP-01 with its Wi-Fi and full TCP/IP stack makes the ESP8266 very popular with makers. The following is a photograph of the ESP-12F, also known as the ESP8266 Wi-Fi Witty Cloud Development board:

Other versions of the ESP-8266 include the ESP-01, ESP-02, and so on.

The ESP-12F features an RGB LED and light sensor. These features allow a developer to easily test out code without having to hook up sensors or LEDs. The ESP-12F may be programmed using the standard Arduino IDE through the removable daughter board that comes with the module.

Arduino

Italian-based Arduino started as a project for students in 2005. This open source microcontroller features digital and analog inputs and outputs and is considered one of the best microcontrollers for beginners. The following is a photograph of the Arduino Uno, which was the first USB-based Arduino board. It features 14 digital I/O pins and 6 analog input pins:

Many expansion boards, called **Shields** in the Arduino world, are available for Arduino boards. These boards include CNC motor control, relay control, touchpads, and Ethernet boards. Arduino boards, such as the Uno, do not have Wi-Fi built in and hence are not the ideal choice for IoT applications.

PyCom boards

PyCom boards simplify IoT development by supplying various methods for connecting to the outside world. PyCom boards utilize the MicroPython microcontroller language based on Python 3. MicroPython runs on what is referred to as bare metal as it is given access to low-level access to inputs and outputs. The following photograph shows the PyCom LoPy board:

It features Bluetooth, LoRa, and Wi-Fi connectivity. We will cover communications protocols in Chapter 3, *Communications Protocols Used in Edge Analytics.* We will also feature the Pycom Lopy in Chapter 6, *Using MicroPython for Edge Analytics.*

The Raspberry Pi

The Raspberry Pi is a single-board computer that exists in various formats. It was developed in the UK and was originally designed to inspire young students to pursue interests in computer science. Since its release in 2012, there have been over 19 million Raspberry Pis sold. Currently, there are 9 different models of the Raspberry Pi sold. These are as follows:

- Raspberry Pi 4 Model B
- Raspberry Pi 3 Model A+
- Raspberry Pi 3 Model B+
- Raspberry Pi 3 Model B
- Raspberry Pi 2 Model B
- Raspberry Pi 1 Model B+
- Raspberry Pi 1 Model A+
- Raspberry Pi Zero W
- Raspberry Pi Zero

Prices start at 5 USD for the Raspberry Pi Zero and go up to 55 USD for the Raspberry Pi 4 Model B with 4 GB of RAM. The following is a picture of the Raspberry Pi 4 Model B with 4 GB of RAM:

The Raspberry Pi has been very popular with many projects, including IoT projects. My previous book, *Internet of Things Programming Projects*, uses the Raspberry Pi exclusively in the building of IoT-based projects including an internet-controlled robot car. As mentioned in `Chapter 1`, *Introduction to Edge Analytics*, the Raspberry Pi 4 Model B has brought the Raspberry Pi to desktop replacement levels. In fact, I am using this same model to write this book.

Personal computers

For real processing power at the edge, we could use a standard PC or server. The makes and models of these computers are too numerous to mention here. However, it's good to know that, if needed on the edge, there is this option.

Microsoft Azure IoT Edge components

The following is a high-level diagram of Microsoft Azure using Azure IoT Edge. As we can see, there are three major components, devices, Azure IoT Edge, and Azure IoT:

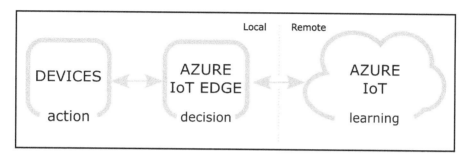

Let's look at devices and Azure IoT Edge in more detail.

Devices

Devices perform actions in Azure IoT Edge. Physically, these devices could be things, such as temperature sensors, laser sensors, and servos. Each device has an associated module registered with it. Modules, however, do not need to have devices associated with them. For example, a TensorFlow model used for object detection would not have a device associated with it. However, it could be used with a module associated with a camera.

Azure IoT Edge

Azure IoT Edge itself is made up of three components. These are as follows:

- IoT Edge modules
- IoT Edge runtime
- A cloud-based interface

Let's take a look at the components of Azure IoT Edge.

IoT Edge modules

IoT Edge modules are execution units that run business logic. They are implemented as Docker compatible containers. Azure IoT edge modules contain Azure services or custom code and are the smallest unit handled by Azure IoT. There are four elements to an IoT edge module. They are as follows:

- Module image
- Module instance
- Module identity
- Module twin

A module image contains applications that use the management, communications and security features of the Azure IoT Edge runtime. A developer may create their own module image or export one from a supported Azure service. Module images exist in the cloud and may be used in different solutions. Every time a module image is deployed to a device, a new module instance is created once the IoT Edge runtime is started. The following diagram shows a module image that lives in the cloud and the deployment of this image in two different geographic locations (Canada and the United Kingdom):

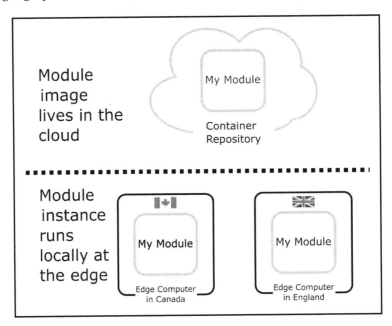

You may deploy multiple module images and put them on any edge computer anywhere in the world. However, each module instance would be its own entity once the module is started.

Module identities are created whenever the Azure IoT Edge runtime creates a new module instance. Module identities are used for local and cloud communications for the module instance. Corresponding module twins are created for each module instance and used to configure the module instance. Module twins and module instances are associated with each other using the module entity. Module twins are JSON documents that store module information and configuration properties.

Azure IoT Edge runtime

The Azure IoT Edge runtime enables logic on IoT edge devices or edge computers. It sits on the edge device or edge computer, such as a Raspberry Pi. It is responsible for several functions:

- It's responsible for the installation and updating of workload on the edge device.
- It's responsible for the maintenance of Azure IoT Edge security standards on the edge device.
- It makes sure that the IoT Edge modules are always running.
- It reports module health for remote monitoring to the cloud.
- It manages communications:
    - Between modules on the Edge device
    - Between the Edge device and the cloud
    - Between downstream devices such as sensors and the Edge device

The following is a diagram of the Azure IoT Edge runtime. As we can see, the runtime acts as a sort of traffic cop for the modules inside the Azure IoT Edge device:

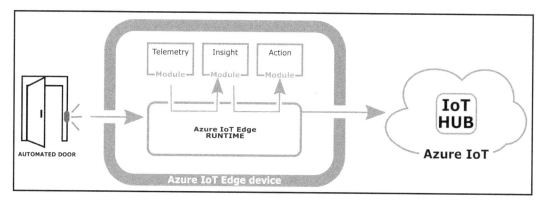

We will work with the Azure IoT Edge runtime when we get hands-on experience with Azure IoT Edge in Chapter 5, *Using the Raspberry Pi with Azure IoT Edge*.

Cloud-based interface

The Azure cloud-based interface allows the user to manage and monitor edge IoT devices.

The cloud service allows us to do the following:

- Creation and configuration of a workload to be run on a specific device
- Sending out a workload to a set of devices
- Monitoring of workloads running on field devices

We will cover more of this in Chapter 4, *Working with Microsoft Azure IoT Hub*, as we get some hands-on experience with Azure IoT Edge.

How do the components fit together?

Connecting our components together physically is similar for both basic edge analytics applications and edge analytics applications based on Microsoft Azure IoT. Input and output pins exist on many of the microcontrollers used for IoT and edge analytics applications. In the coming sections, we will outline how this done.

Connecting a sensor to the ESP-12F microcontroller

The following diagram shows a weather predictor I built using the ESP-12F module. Although it is not an edge analytics application per se, it does show how to connect a microcontroller to an LED and the internet. The weather predictor uses barometric pressure values taken for a web service to determine whether there will be good weather coming:

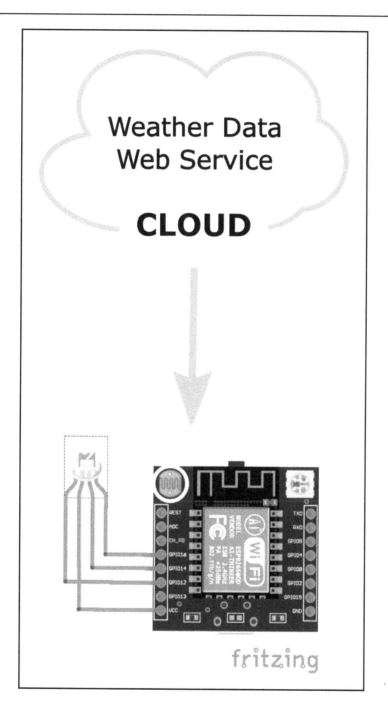

As you can see in the diagram, an RGB LED is connected to the GPIO ports on the ESP-12F. The type of RGB LED used in this circuit has a common anode. Hence, the RGB LED is connected as follows:

- Red cathode to GPIO12
- Common anode to VCC
- Green cathode to GPIO14
- Blue cathode to GPIO16

 To use this application, you must sign up for an Open Weather Map account at www.openweathermap.com and obtain an API key.

The following code written in C is for the weather predictor:

```c
#include <ESP8266WiFi.h>
#include <WiFiClient.h>
#include <OpenWeatherMap.h>

const char *ow_key = "XXXXXXXXXXXXXXXXXXX";
const char *ssid = "XXXXX";
const char *pass = "XXXXXXXXX";
OWMconditions owCC;
float press_old=0;
float press_new;
bool high_press_flag = false;
bool initialize = false;
#define GREEN_LED 14
#define BLUE_LED 16
#define RED_LED 12

void setup() {
    Serial.begin(9600);
    delay(10);
    Wi-Fi.softAPdisconnect (true);
    pinMode(GREEN_LED, OUTPUT);
    pinMode(BLUE_LED, OUTPUT);
    pinMode(RED_LED, OUTPUT);
}

void currentConditions(void) {
    OWM_conditions *ow_cond = new OWM_conditions;
    owCC.updateConditions(ow_cond, ow_key, "ca", "Toronto", "metric");
    press_new = ow_cond->pressure.toFloat();
```

```
   if (press_new > 0)
   {
      if (press_old == 0)
      {
         press_old = press_new;
      }
      if (press_new != press_old)
      {
        initialize = true;
        if (press_new > press_old)
         {
             high_press_flag = true;
         }
         else
         {
             high_press_flag = false;
         }
         press_old = press_new;
      }
   }

   delete ow_cond;
}

void loop() {
       if (Wi-Fi.status() != WL_CONNECTED) { //wifi not connected?
            Wi-Fi.begin(ssid, pass);
            Serial.println("Connecting to Wi-Fi");
            delay(2000);
            if (Wi-Fi.waitForConnectResult() == WL_CONNECTED) {
                Serial.println("Wi-Fi Connected!");
                delay(2000);
                return;
            }
       }
       if (Wi-Fi.waitForConnectResult() == WL_CONNECTED) {
                currentConditions();
                if (initialize == true)
                {
                  if (high_press_flag == true)
                  {
                      FlashGreenLED(250, 5);
                  }
                  else
                  {
                      FlashRedLED(100, 10);
                  }
                }
```

```
                    else
                    {
                            FlashBlueLED(500, 5);
                    }
                    if (press_new > 0)
                    {
                        delay(900000);
                    }
                    else
                    {    .
                        delay(10000);
                    }
                    return;
            }
    }

    void FlashGreenLED(int delayTime, int numOfFlashes) {
        int var = 0;
        while(var < numOfFlashes ) {
            digitalWrite(BLUE_LED, LOW);
            digitalWrite(RED_LED, LOW);
            digitalWrite(GREEN_LED, LOW);
            delay(delayTime);
            digitalWrite(GREEN_LED, HIGH);
            delay(delayTime);
            var++;
        }
    }

    void FlashBlueLED(int delayTime, int numOfFlashes) {
        int var = 0;
        while(var < numOfFlashes ) {
            digitalWrite(GREEN_LED, LOW);
            digitalWrite(RED_LED, LOW);
            digitalWrite(BLUE_LED, LOW);
            delay(delayTime);
            digitalWrite(BLUE_LED, HIGH);
            delay(delayTime);
            var++;
        }
    }

    void FlashRedLED(int delayTime, int numOfFlashes) {
        int var = 0;
        while(var < numOfFlashes ) {
            digitalWrite(GREEN_LED, LOW);
            digitalWrite(BLUE_LED, LOW);
            digitalWrite(RED_LED, LOW);
```

```
        delay(delayTime);
        digitalWrite(RED_LED, HIGH);
        delay(delayTime);
        var++;
    }
}
```

 Barometers are scientific instruments used to measure barometric pressure. Changes in barometric pressure are good indicators of short-term weather changes. A drop in pressure, for example, indicates that a low-pressure system is coming, which means rain and wind.

Our code starts off by including the necessary libraries:

```
#include <ESP8266WiFi.h>
#include <WiFiClient.h>
#include <OpenWeatherMap.h>
```

We then set up the variables used in our code:

```
const char *ow_key = "XXXXXXXXXXXXXXXXXXXX";
const char *ssid = "XXXXX";
const char *pass = "XXXXXXXXX";
OWMconditions owCC;
float press_old=0;
float press_new;
bool high_press_flag = false;
bool initialize = false;
#define GREEN_LED 14
#define BLUE_LED 16
#define RED_LED 12
```

The *ow_key constant is obtained when we set up an account with Open Weather. The *ssid and *pass constants are the SSID and password for our Wi-Fi router respectively. We use the owCC variable to call the Open Weather Map web service later in the code. press_old and press_new are float values we use to determine whether the barometric pressure is rising or falling. The high_press_flag is set high in the code once it has been determined that the pressure is rising. The initialize flag is used to indicate whether an initial state has been determined (barometric pressure is rising or falling).

We then set the pin numbers of the ESP-12F to the colors of the RGB LED that they are wired to as shown in the preceding diagram.

Our `setup()` method sets the baud rate (for using the Arduino serial monitor in troubleshooting) to 9600. A delay of 10 milliseconds is set. Our code then turns off the microcontroller's Wi-Fi AP mode (so you won't see it pop up in a list of local Wi-Fi routers) before the `GREEN_LED`, `BLUE_LED`, and `RED_LED` values are set to `OUTPUT`:

```
void setup() {
    Serial.begin(9600);
    delay(10);
    Wi-Fi.softAPdisconnect (true);
    pinMode(GREEN_LED, OUTPUT);
    pinMode(BLUE_LED, OUTPUT);
    pinMode(RED_LED, OUTPUT);
}
```

The `currentConditions()` method is where all of the magic happens. It is here where we call the Open Weather Map web service using the `owCC.updateConditions()` method of the `OWM_conditions` variable, `*ow_cond`. We acquired access to the `OWM_conditions` object when we included `OpenWeatherMap.h` at the top of our code.

In our code, we are using the Open Weather Map web service to pull out barometric pressure for Toronto, Canada. We assign the `press_new` variable to the barometric pressure reading we acquire from the web service:

```
void currentConditions(void) {
    OWM_conditions *ow_cond = new OWM_conditions;
    owCC.updateConditions(ow_cond, ow_key, "ca", "Toronto", "metric");
    press_new = ow_cond->pressure.toFloat();

    if (press_new > 0)
    {
        if (press_old == 0)
        {
            press_old = press_new;
        }
        if (press_new != press_old)
        {
            initialize = true;
            if (press_new > press_old)
            {
                high_press_flag = true;
            }
            else
            {
                high_press_flag = false;
            }
            press_old = press_new;
```

```
        }
    }

    delete ow_cond;
}
```

We then perform a series of logic tests to determine whether the barometric pressure is rising or falling. If this is our first reading, we keep the `initialize` flag at `false` (by not setting it to `true`) as we are not yet ready to determine a rising or falling barometric pressure. It may take a few hours before a rising or falling barometric pressure has been determined.

Our `loop()` method checks the Wi-Fi connection before proceeding. What follows is a series of logic tests to determine which light to flash:

```
void loop() {
    if (Wi-Fi.status() != WL_CONNECTED) { //wifi not connected?
        Wi-Fi.begin(ssid, pass);
        Serial.println("Connecting to Wi-Fi");
        delay(2000);
        if (Wi-Fi.waitForConnectResult() == WL_CONNECTED) {
            Serial.println("Wi-Fi Connected!");
            delay(2000);
            return;
        }
    }
    if (Wi-Fi.waitForConnectResult() == WL_CONNECTED) {
        currentConditions();
        if (initialize == true)
        {
          if (high_press_flag == true)
          {
              FlashGreenLED(250, 5);
          }
          else
          {
              FlashRedLED(100, 10);
          }
        }
        else
        {
              FlashBlueLED(500, 5);
        }
        if (press_new > 0)
        {
              delay(900000);
        }
```

```
            else
            {
                delay(10000);
            }
            return;
        }
    }
```

The `FlashGreenLED()`, `FlashBlueLED()`, and `FlashRedLED()` methods are pretty self-explanatory. As you can tell in the logic, we flash the green LED when the barometric pressure is rising, the red LED when the barometric pressure is falling, and the blue LED before it has been determined whether the barometric pressure is rising or falling. Looking at the code to flash the LED (which we will not repeat), we can see that we end the flashing with a high state. This means that the LED will flash for a short time before remaining either green, red, or blue.

Now that we have a basic understanding of how to connect a component, let's take a look at more real-world edge analytics examples.

More examples of real-world edge analytics applications

Japan's Komatsu is a global manufacturer of construction machinery. Worker shortage is a major issue for Komatsu. To address this, they developed a smart factory platform called **KOM-MICS**.

KOM-MICS smart factory platform

KOM-MICS uses Azure services and Windows tablets (edge devices) to collect and analyze data from machine tools and robots to drive efficiencies. The data collected is stored and then processed in the Azure cloud. This processed data is then sent back to Windows PCs where a custom viewer and Microsoft Power BI are utilized.

Services from Azure are implemented in the cloud. Instead of utilizing their own servers and IT software and services, Komatsu uses a virtual machine from Microsoft. As well, cloud-based file storage and database from Microsoft are implemented. This allows Komatsu to offload the maintenance and security of IT infrastructure and services to Microsoft.

You may be asking yourself, where does the edge analytics aspect come into play? Without a more in-depth understanding of KOM-MICS, it's hard to say how much processing is handled on the edge side of the smart factory application. However, the most important idea to take from this example is the use of Azure. We will be looking into the use of Azure services when we start to look a little more deeply into Azure IoT Edge.

The efficiencies that come from KOM-MICS allow Komatsu to better handle the challenges of their marketplace.

Summary

In this chapter, we introduced components used in building an edge analytics application. We touched on the venerable DHT-11 temperature and humidity sensor. We outlined how it may be set up with a Raspberry Pi. We also touched on some Python code to demonstrate how this sensor may be used in an application.

For smart garden type applications, the soil moisture sensor is the key component. We looked at this sensor and described what a smart garden edge analytics application would look like. We also took a brief look at security applications by discussing the laser sensor.

Edge analytics wouldn't be possible without some sort of edge device and we explored a few of them by looking at various microcontrollers and computers used. We then dug into what makes up Azure IoT Edge by looking at the software components of this platform.

In our section on describing how the components fit together, we viewed a weather predictor application using an ESP8266 type microcontroller. From this application, we learned how to wire up and write code for sensors.

We concluded our chapter by looking at another example of how edge analytics is used in the real world by examining the KOM-MICS smart factory platform.

In the next chapter, we will look at the communication protocols used in edge analytics.

Questions

Having learned the lessons in this chapter, try answering the following questions on your own:

1. True/False. Sensors are an important part of an edge analytics application.
2. True/False. The DHT11 sensor is used to measure distance.
3. How many parts make up a soil moisture sensor?
4. What is a *smart garden*?
5. True/False. Albert Einstein had something to do with the development of the laser.
6. What year did the ESP8266 chip receive critical attention?
7. True/False. Arduino started as a project for students in 2005.
8. What does the Azure IoT Edge runtime enable?
9. True/False. A module image lives in the cloud.
10. True/False. With our weather predictor application, a blue LED indicates that a rising or falling barometric pressure has not been determined.

Further reading

Check out the Microsoft website, `https://customers.microsoft.com`, for more information on how Azure IoT Edge and Azure IoT are used in real-world scenarios.

3
Communications Protocols Used in Edge Analytics

One part of an IoT or edge analytics application is the connection to the internet. The other part is the connection of our edge device to the sensors. In this chapter, we will explore ways to connect our edge device to the internet. We will look at some of the long-distance technologies as well as the familiar Wi-Fi protocol. In our exploration of Wi-Fi, we will gain an understanding of the RF spectrum and where different communication protocols fit into this spectrum. As well, we will take a look at Bluetooth and how we may use it in our applications.

In this chapter, we will cover the following:

- Wi-Fi communication for edge analytics
- Bluetooth for edge analytics communication
- Cellular technologies for edge analytics communication
- Long-distance communication using LoRa and Sigfox for edge analytics

Wi-Fi communication for edge analytics

Wireless communication is probably the most common technology used for IoT and edge analytics applications. We generally use Wi-Fi to connect our edge computer or microcontroller to a router for internet access.

Wi-Fi uses the IEEE 802.11 protocol and transmits with channels divided in the radio frequency ranges in and around 900 MHz, 2.4 GHz, 3.6 GHz, 4.9 GHz, 5 GHz, 5.9 GHz, and 60 GHz. The 2.4 GHz and 5 GHz frequencies are the most common.

To get a better understanding of what these frequencies mean, let's take a look at the radio frequency or RF spectrum.

Understanding the RF spectrum

Invisible radio waves are all around us. We take them for granted. To understand wireless communications, in general, it is a good idea to take a look at the radio frequency spectrum. The following diagram is a graphic describing this spectrum:

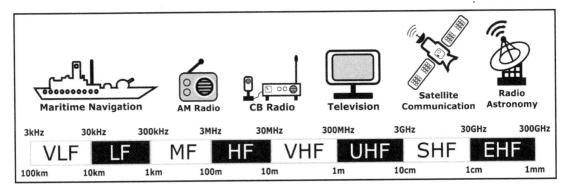

As you can see, there are frequencies ranging from 3 kHz all the way up to 300 GHz. The corresponding wavelengths are shown at the bottom of the graphic. The RF spectrum is subdivided into the following bands:

- **VLF**: Very low frequency
- **LF**: Low frequency
- **MF**: Medium frequency
- **HF**: High frequency
- **VHF**: Very high frequency
- **UHF**: Ultra-high frequency
- **SHF**: Super high frequency
- **EHF**: Extremely high frequency

Let's take a deeper look at each of the frequency bands.

VLF and LF

VLF sits in the 3 kHz to 30 kHz range in the RF spectrum with wavelengths from 100 km to 10 km respectively. Due to the relatively large wavelengths of VLF signals, the reflection of the signal is limited. This makes the VLF band useful for marine applications such as submarines. The following diagram illustrates this concept:

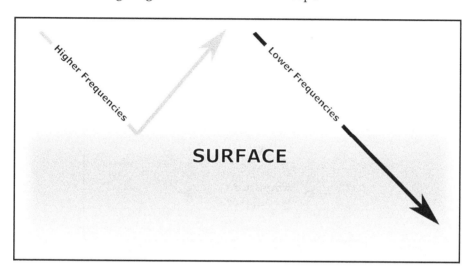

As you can see in the preceding diagram, lower frequencies penetrate surfaces better than higher frequencies. Think of the night club playing loud music. It is the lower frequencies that you hear the most when standing outside the club.

Sitting in the 30 kHz to 300 kHz range with wavelengths between 10 km and 1 km is the Low Frequency or LF band. Military and amateur radio operators use this band for communications. Some **Radio Frequency Identification** (**RFID**) tags and readers operate in the 125-134 kHz range due to the ability of low frequencies to penetrate objects.

Medium frequency

The medium frequency band sits between 300 kHz and 3 MHz with wavelengths of 1 km and 100 m respectively. One of the most popular applications using this frequency range is AM radio. AM radio is based on technology developed in the early 1900s and saw widespread adoption in the 1920s.

Have you ever listened to the radio and wondered what the number representing the radio station meant? In Toronto, Canada, for example, there is a radio station on the AM band called 680 News. The 680 actually refers to the frequency that is used to broadcast this station, 680 kHz:

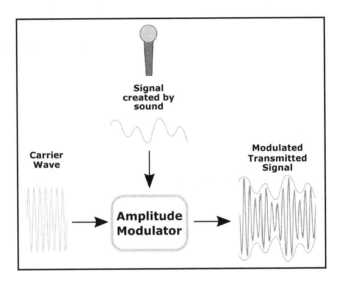

The AM in AM radio stands for amplitude modulation, a method of modulating a radio wave where the amplitude of the carrier wave is modulated proportionally to the message signal. As we can see in the preceding diagram, the Amplitude Modulator modulates the carrier wave based on the sound coming from the sound source (microphone).

AM radio broadcasts in the 535 kHz to 1605 kHz range with stations assigned from 540 kHz in intervals of 10 kHz.

High frequency

The high frequency band sits between 3 MHz and 30 MHz with wavelengths of 100 m and 10 m respectively. A prominent application using the HF range is CB, or Citizen's Band, a radio that operates with 40 channels near the 27 MHz frequency. The popularity of CB radio peaked in the late 1970s to the early 1980s in what could be described as a pre-internet version of chat room talk:

Many users of CB radio take advantage of a phenomenon known as *skip* to achieve long-distance communications with their transceivers. Skip occurs when radio signals skip off of the ionosphere, a layer of the upper atmosphere that is electrically charged, to locations great distances away. The distance covered with this method depends on things, such as the time of day and solar flare activity on the sun.

Very high frequency

The very high frequency band sits between 30 MHz to 300 MHz with wavelengths from 10 m to 1 m respectively and is one of the most used frequency bands. VHF is used for TV broadcasting as well as FM radio. FM radio operates in the 88 MHz to 108 MHz range of the VHF band.

Airline pilots communicate with air traffic controllers using the 118 MHz to 137 MHz range of the VHF band.

Ultra high frequency

The UHF band sits in the 300 MHz to 3 GHz range with wavelengths of 1 m to 10 cm. UHF is arguably the most important frequency band for modern communications. Applications using this band include television, GPS, pagers, Wi-Fi, Bluetooth, and GSM and LTE cellular communications.

As antenna size is dependent on wavelength, antennas used for UHF television reception are smaller than ones used for VHF (outlined in the following screenshot):

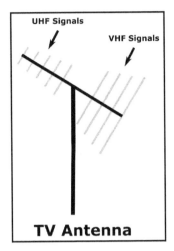

Many Wi-Fi routers operate at channels in the 2.4 GHz range although 5 GHz (in the SHF band) is becoming more popular. We will look at the difference between 2.4 GHz Wi-Fi and 5 GHz Wi-Fi in the section *What is bandwidth?*.

Super high frequency

The SHF band sits in the 3 GHz to 30 GHz range with wavelengths of 10 m to 1 cm. Due to its small wavelength, SHF is limited to line of sight direct communications such as satellite to satellite communication. Wi-Fi routers that use the 5 GHz frequency have a shorter range than ones that used 2.4 GHz. So, why would you want to use a 5 GHz Wi-Fi router instead of a 2.4 GHz router? We will explain this in the upcoming *What is bandwidth?* section.

Extremely high frequency

The EHF band sits in the 30 GHz to 300 GHz range with wavelengths of 1 cm and 1 mm. It is used for more advanced communication such as radio telescopes. 5G networks aim to take advantage of the speed offered by the EHF frequency band.

What is bandwidth?

When researching communications technologies for your edge analytics applications, the term *bandwidth* is mentioned quite a bit. So what exactly is bandwidth?

There are actually two different meanings of bandwidth when it comes to communications technology—an analog version and a digital version. For the analog world, bandwidth is simply a range of frequencies within a band. For example, CB radio has a bandwidth of 26.9650 MHz to 27.4050 MHz divided into 40 channels in the HF frequency band. CB channel 19 in both Canada and the United States uses the frequency 27.185 MHz.

On the digital side, bandwidth refers to the amount of data that a device can transmit in a certain amount of time measured in bits per second, or bps. We can think of it like cars traveling on a highway with the cars representing the data. If we were to increase the number of lanes on the highway, we would increase the number of cars that can travel on it or our bandwidth. As well, we may also increase our bandwidth when we increase the speed of our highway. Consider the following diagram:

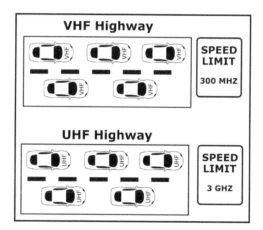

Please note that all radio waves move at the speed of light. A VHF signal will travel at the same speed as a UHF signal. The speed we are referring to in the preceding diagram is the time taken for the radio wave to complete one cycle. As the wavelength decreases when frequency increases, shorter waves will cycle more quickly than longer waves.

In the following diagram, we can see that the wavelength of a UHF wave is shorter than the wavelength of a VHF wave. The result is more cycles in a fixed amount of time (1 second) for the UHF waves as compared to the VHF waves:

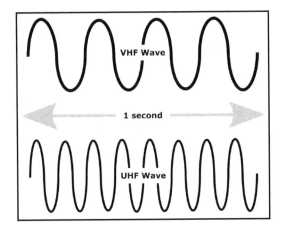

As we asked the question why would we want to use 5 GHz Wi-Fi router over a 2.4 GHz one, we can see in the preceding diagrams, the higher the frequency, the higher the speed at which data may be transmitted.

Using Wi-Fi for our edge analytics applications

Now that we have a better understanding of wireless communications, let's take a look at how we would incorporate Wi-Fi into our edge analytics applications. In the following diagram, we will design a smart heating system for an ice rink:

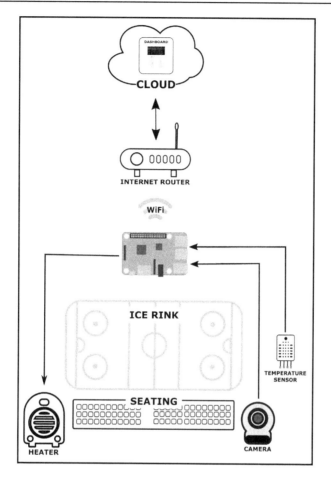

For a country of 37 million people, Canada boasts over 3,000 indoor skating rinks. You will easily find a rink in almost every small town and neighborhood. A common complaint among patrons of ice rinks is how cold it is in the stands. Many rinks have heaters above the seats; however, knowing when to turn on the heat or keep it shut off to save on energy bills is a decision that needs to be constantly made.

Our preceding smart heater edge analytics application promises to fix this. Using a temperature sensor and a camera for image recognition, our application checks the temperature and scans for people in the seats. It can turn on the heaters when the vision recognition software determines that there are a certain number of people in the seats. It can then turn on the heater and maintain a certain temperature using the temperature sensor. The operation of the application is done through our edge device, in this case, a Raspberry Pi computer. A cloud-based dashboard is updated through the internet.

We can see that our edge device is connected using Wi-Fi to the internet router. Wi-Fi is the best option for communicating to the router, and in turn, the internet, as rinks tend to have Wi-Fi access throughout. We would use 5 GHz Wi-Fi instead of 2.4 GHz, as ice rinks tend to have open designs due to the size of the ice. There are only a few objects to interrupt our Wi-Fi signal.

Let's now take a look at Bluetooth, a technology designed for short-distance communications, and see how we may incorporate this concept into our edge analytics applications.

Bluetooth for edge analytics communication

We use Wi-Fi to connect our edge device to an internet router to gain access to the internet. But what about the connections from our edge device to our sensors? So far, we have shown these connections to be made via a wire hooked up to the **General Purpose Input Output** (**GPIO**) port of our edge device to our sensors or switches. However, there is a way to hook up devices wirelessly to our edge device. One such technology is Bluetooth. In the following sections, we will discuss this technology and display how it may be used in an edge analytics application.

What is Bluetooth?

Designed as a wireless alternative to data cables, Bluetooth operates in the UHF band of frequencies from 2.400 to 2.485 GHz. The idea of short-link radio technology was first devised in 1989 with the first commercial application coming ten years later in the form of a hands-free headset for a mobile phone. The range of a Bluetooth device depends on its class. The following is a table of these classes. The ranges are approximate:

Class	Transmission Power	Range
1	100 mW	100 meters
2	2.5 mW	10 meters
3	1 mW	1 meter

Enhancing our smart heater application with Bluetooth

Incorporating Bluetooth technology into our edge analytics designs is somewhat limiting due to the range. However, there is an app available for the Android operating system called **Blue Dot** that may be quite useful for our designs. Blue Dot features a big blue dot on the screen that may be pressed, double pressed, swiped, and so on. It is designed to work with the Raspberry Pi. The following diagram shows our hockey rink smart heater modified to use Blue Dot on a tablet as a remote control:

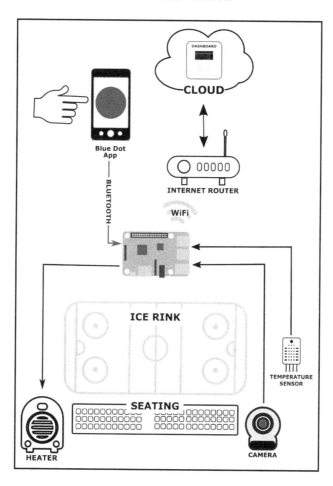

As you can see, we've added the Blue Dot app to our design. We can use finger gestures to control our heater, overriding the temperature sensor and camera if we choose. For example, we may use a double-tap to turn off the heater regardless of how many people are seated.

Cellular technologies for edge analytics communication

For edge analytics applications where access to a Wi-Fi-connected internet router is available, connection to the outside world is relatively simple. For more remote applications, other types of communications technologies are required. We will look at some of those technologies in the remaining sections of this chapter. We will first start with cellular data and explain the importance of 5G technology for IoT and edge analytics.

The generations of cellular network technology

Cellular phones and devices use frequencies starting in the UHF band with bandwidth (the analog version of bandwidth) regionally dependent. Motorola launched the first commercial cell phone in 1983. It cost thousands of dollars and had a short battery life. Since that time cellular phone technology has improved by leaps and bounds. The following diagram shows the different phases of cellular network technology:

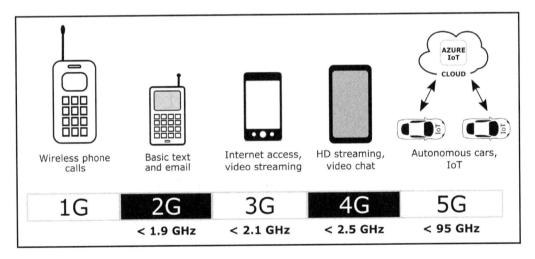

The **G** in the different phases represents the **generation** of the technology. As you can see, applications requiring faster and faster network connections and more and more processing power follow the progression of the technology. Also, higher transmission frequencies are required for each subsequent generation, with a significant jump for 5G. Of note is the positioning of 5G technology for use in IoT applications. Let's take a look at 5G and how it would benefit IoT and edge analytics applications.

What is 5G?

5G represents the latest in cellular network technology. For IoT solutions, it incorporates frequencies as high 95 GHz (the EHF frequency band). Transmission is divided up among small cell towers using multiple antennas. Due to the fact that small wavelengths have shorter ranges than larger wavelengths (lower frequencies) a method called **beamforming** is incorporated into 5G, as shown in the following diagram:

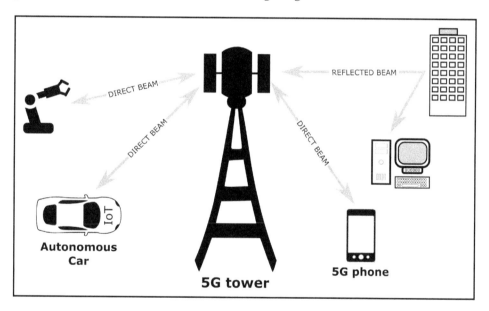

With beamforming, signals are sent directly to 5G devices from 5G mini-towers. As higher frequencies reflect easily off of solid objects, reflected beams will also be used in 5G beamforming. Beamforming allows for low latency links between devices using the same tower. This would be useful, for example, in **Vehicle-to-Vehicle** (**V2V**) communications for self-driving cars.

How would 5G enhance our edge analytics applications?

Higher bandwidth and lower latency are improvements to any network application. In the case of our edge analytics applications, the ability to communicate quickly with other edge devices allows us to build applications very sensitive to time, such as robotics applications. However, the whole point of edge analytics is to move processing to the edge to gain improvements in speed and reliability. Cellular communication may not be worth the cost if our edge analytics application only needs to send data to the cloud periodically.

For cost savings, there are other technologies that may be better suited to our edge analytics applications. We will go over some of these technologies in the next section.

Long-distance communication using LoRa and Sigfox for edge analytics

For remote edge analytics or IoT applications, power consumption and signal range are important factors. As we've seen, 5G offers amazing data transfer rates and low latency, however, the range of 5G and cellular network technology, in general, is limited. Using a lower frequency and sacrificing data bandwidth may be a good option for our remote edge analytics and IoT applications. In the case of edge analytics, it may be the best option.

Two technologies designed for remote edge analytics and IoT applications are LoRa and Sigfox. We will take a look at both of these technologies in this section. Before we do though, let's discuss the Friis transmission formula equation and use it to back up the argument of using lower frequencies for communications.

The Friis transmission equation

First presented by radio engineer Harald T. Friis in 1946, the Friis transmission equation is used to equate the power received at the end of an antenna. The following diagram shows the Friis transmission equation. For the purposes of our discussion, we will look at received power, transmitted power, the distance between antennas, and wavelength:

$$P_r = \frac{P_t\, G_t\, G_r\, \lambda^2}{(4\pi)^2 d^2}$$

P_r = received power		P_t = transmitted power	
G_t = transmitter antenna gain		G_r = receiver antenna gain	
d = distance between antennas		λ = wavelength	

As we can see from the equation, the received power decreases exponentially with the distance between the antennas. To compensate for that, we need to increase the transmitted power between the two antennas. For our remote edge analytics applications, ones that may for example run on solar power, increasing transmitted power may not be that easy. As well, we may only require limited messaging between the remote location and a base station. Remember, one of the reasons that we chose to design our IoT applications as edge analytics applications is to reduce the amount of network traffic and process data close to the *edge*.

Looking at the Friis equation again we can see that received power increases exponentially with wavelength. So, in other words, when our wavelength increases, so does the power received exponentially. Wavelength increases as frequency decreases, therefore to increase power received we could decrease the transmission frequency.

Two technologies that use lower frequencies designed for IoT applications are Sigfox and LoRa. Let's take a look at both of these technologies.

Sigfox

Founded in 2009, Sigfox is a French-based wireless IoT services company. Applications such as smartwatches, parking sensors, and gas and electricity meters use the Sigfox service. Sigfox has global coverage and operates in the 868 MHz (Europe) and 902 MHz (United States) unlicensed radio frequencies. Sigfox owns and operates the Sigfox network.

Sigfox is considered a **Low-Power Wide-Area Network** (**LPWAN**) technology. LPWAN is a technology designed for long-range communications with low digital bandwidth.

LoRa and LoRaWAN

Another long-range communications technology for IoT and edge analytics is LoRa and its WAN version, LoRaWAN. **LoRa** simply stands for **Long Range** and **LoRaWAN** for **Long-Range Wide Area Network**. LoRa operates in the UHF frequency bands with frequencies of 433 MHz (Asia), 868 MHz (Europe), and 915 MHz (North America). Unlike Sigfox, anyone can make their own LoRaWAN network by buying appropriate hardware. The following diagram is an example of using a LoRa Gateway to connect devices with LoRa transceivers to the internet using either Wi-Fi, cellular data (3G or 4G), or Ethernet:

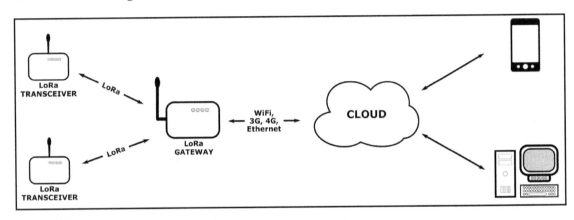

The following photograph shows an actual LoRa Gateway device, the Dragino LG-01:

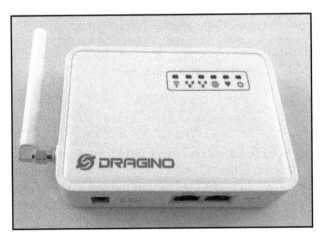

LoRa networks using such a system as the preceding may see ranges of up to 10 km, all the while requiring a low amount of power. We will be using LoRa in a project in Chapter 6, *Using MicroPython for Edge Analytics*.

Summary

We covered quite a bit in this chapter starting with a look at the frequency spectrum and continuing with a discussion on some of the communications technologies we may use in our edge analytics applications.

Understanding how frequency, transmission range, and bandwidth work together is essential in deciding on the technologies to use for our applications. By far the easiest and most widely used communications technology is Wi-Fi. It is ideal if our application is able to connect to a Wi-Fi source to gain access to the internet. For more remote edge analytics applications, other technologies must be looked at such as cellular and LoRa.

Questions

Having learned the lessons in this chapter, try answering the following questions on your own:

1. True/False. Wi-Fi is the most common communications technology used for edge analytics applications.
2. True/False. VLF and LF frequency bands are used for marine communications applications.
3. What is the frequency used for CB channel 19 in Canada and the United States?
4. What is meant by bandwidth in the analog world of communications?
5. True/False. Wavelength decreases as frequency increases.
6. What is the range of Bluetooth class 1?
7. True/False. Basic text and email was possible with 2G cellular technologies.
8. What does LPWAN stand for?
9. True/False. Received power increases exponentially when wavelength increases.
10. True/False. It is possible to get a 10 km range using LoRa technology.

Further reading

Looking back on past technologies provides an appreciation for the amazing technologies we enjoy today. A book that did that for me was *The Big Dummy's Guide to C.B. Radio*, a paperback from 1976.

Section 2: Understanding Edge Analytics Technologies

2

In order to design new applications with edge analytics, we need to understand the what and how of the IoT ingredients needed. In *Section 2*, we will discuss the technologies and components used to create an edge analytics application. We will learn about Microsoft Azure IoT Edge, AWS IoT Greengrass, MicroPython, and the OpenCV visual recognition library. We will conclude section two by designing a smart doorbell system using some of the technologies we will have learned about.

This section comprises the following chapters:

- Chapter 4, *Working with Microsoft Azure IoT Hub*
- Chapter 5, *Using the Raspberry Pi with Azure IoT Edge*
- Chapter 6, *Using MicroPython for Edge Analytics*
- Chapter 7, *Machine Learning and Edge Analytics*
- Chapter 8, *Designing a Smart Doorbell with Visual Recognition*

4
Working with Microsoft Azure IoT Hub

In `Chapter 1`, *Introduction to Edge Analytics*, we touched on Azure IoT Edge and Azure IoT. In this chapter, we will start to work with Azure IoT services using Microsoft Azure. The lessons learned from this will provide a good background for `Chapter 5`, *Using the Raspberry Pi with Azure IoT Edge*.

We will create a Microsoft Azure account and then proceed to log in to the Azure portal. We will take a brief look at the portal and move on to creating an IoT hub resource. We will transmit simulated data to the IoT hub from a Python client and view it using a Microsoft utility called **Device Explorer**.

In this chapter, we will cover the following topics:

- What is Microsoft Azure?
- What is Azure IoT Hub?
- A quick tutorial on Azure IoT Hub

What is Microsoft Azure?

While attending a webinar on Microsoft Azure, I requested a short description of Microsoft Azure from my host. Here is the response that I received:

> *Microsoft Azure is a cloud computing service created by Microsoft for building, testing, deploying, and managing applications and services through Microsoft-managed data centers. It is a collection of these services to cover a wide range of technology needs.*

To better understand Microsoft Azure, let's expand on the topic of cloud computing as discussed in `Chapter 1`, *Introduction to Edge Analytics*, and focus on cloud service providers, such as Microsoft, and their offerings.

Cloud service providers

Cloud service providers offer users the computer storage and computer processing they require at the time that they require it. A power plant is a good analogy for what cloud service providers offer. The following diagram illustrates this concept:

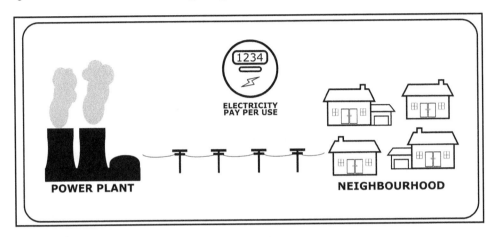

As we can see, the power plant generates electricity and the electricity is sent out on power lines for use by customers. Customers pay only for the electricity they use. The power company is responsible for providing a steady flow of electricity when it is needed. The power company is also responsible for building and maintaining the power plant and keeping it up to date. It would be impractical for the electricity customers to build and maintain their own power plants.

 An exception to this is the houses and buildings equipped with solar panels. As the price of solar panels drops, more and more houses are having them installed on their roofs. In Australia, a continent well-suited to solar energy, it is estimated that 20 percent of homes have solar panels installed on their roofs.

The same parallels apply to cloud service providers. Instead of buying and maintaining servers and a space to run them in, cloud service providers take care of this. In a cloud computing setup, customers pay only for the computing resources they need, just like the way they pay for electricity.

The two main uses for cloud computing are **storage** and **processing**. Let's take a look at how cloud computing provides these services.

Storage

Storing files such as documents and videos is one of the most important functions of a computer. Traditionally, this has been done on a local computer's hard drive. As more files are added, more storage is required. This usually involves buying more hard drives or other types of storage media.

Pushing storage to the cloud frees us up from having to purchase and maintain physical media. Cloud storage, as offered by cloud service providers, takes care of this. Cloud service storage is currently offered by companies such as Dropbox, Google, and Microsoft.

Processing

Offloading computer processing needs is another service provided by cloud service providers. Customers may use as much or as little processing power as they require and only pay for usage. There are three popular options for offloading our processing to the cloud. They are as follows:

- Virtual machines
- Containers
- Serverless computing

Let's take a look at each one of those options in more detail.

Virtual machines

Virtual machines are probably the easiest to understand. A virtual machine is like having your own physical computer or server to install whichever operating system and applications you would like. However, a virtual machine is not a physical machine itself. It is an emulation of a single computer running on a much more powerful computer. The computer that hosts the virtual machine may host many more virtual machines that each operate as if they were a separate computer.

In the following diagram, we can see multiple virtual machines sharing the same hardware:

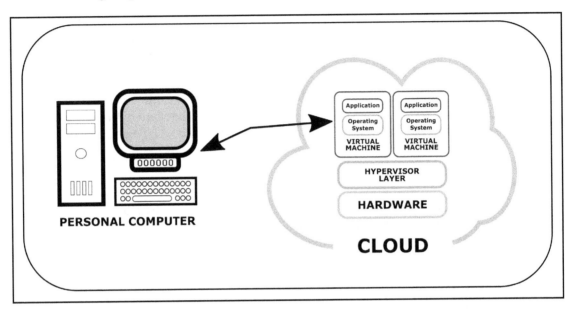

A hypervisor layer, responsible for creating and running the virtual machines, sits over the hardware layer.

A virtual machine is easy to set up and eliminates the hardware costs associated with setting up physical servers. With a virtual machine, the user is responsible for the maintenance and installation of software just as if it were a physical machine.

Containers

Containers are similar to virtual machines with the exception of not having to install a separate operating system. This makes containers quick to implement and lightweight. Many more containers may exist on a physical server than virtual machines can. An application and all of the dependencies required for the application are stored in the container. In the following diagram, we can see how containers share an operating system through the use of a container engine:

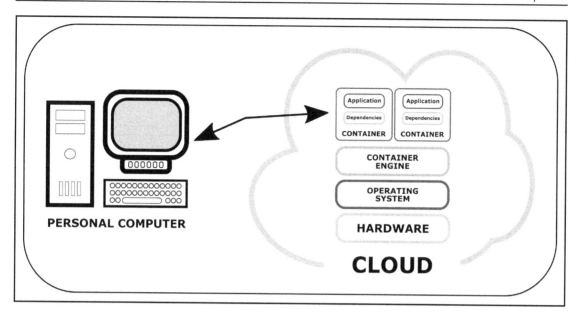

 Docker, an open source project first released in 2013, is one of the most popular container platforms on the market. Docker is available for all of the major operating systems including Windows, macOS, and Linux. A typical use of Docker is the development of WordPress websites for use in deployment to production environments. Check out `www.docker.com` for more information and documentation.

Containers may be easily moved from machine to machine, hence allowing a developer to create an application on a development machine and port it to a hosting machine without the worry of compatibility issues.

Serverless computing

Unlike containers or virtual machines, serverless computing offers users a pay-as-you-go cost structure. Customers of a serverless computing cloud service only pay when the function required is executed in the cloud. The following diagram illustrates a serverless computing system:

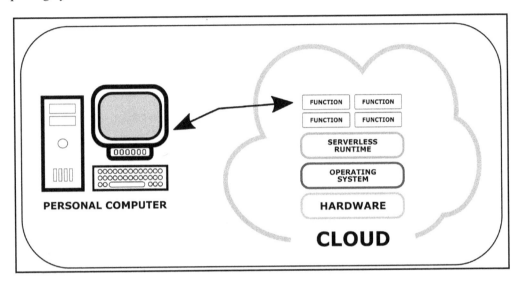

Although it is called serverless, physical servers are indeed used. However, customers need not worry about the underlying hardware and resources.

Serverless computing works well for functions that are stateless and event driven.

A look at Microsoft Azure

This brings us back to Microsoft Azure. With Microsoft Azure, you may rent a virtual machine, deploy your application in a container, or call functions such as a machine learning algorithm. Microsoft Azure achieves this through four categories of cloud computing. These are as follows:

- **IaaS**: Infrastructure as a service
- **PaaS:** Platform as a service
- **SaaS:** Software as a service
- **FaaS**: Functions as a service

Let's take a look at each one of these categories.

Infrastructure as a service

IaaS offers the most flexibility. Think of virtual machines as an IaaS offering. The user is responsible for managing and maintaining the operating system and applications. In the following diagram, we can see that the actual physical machines, databases, and networking are handled by Microsoft. As well, Microsoft handles the virtualization of the virtual machine (through the use of a hypervisor):

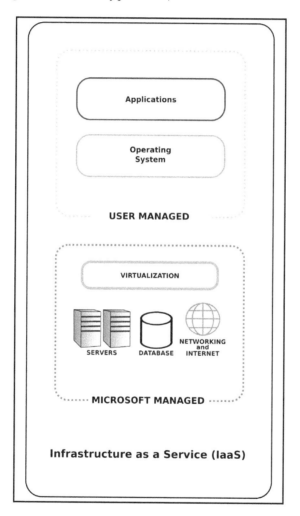

IaaS is a way of renting a server as opposed to buying a physical one. Common usages for IaaS is the migration of on-premises computing resources and for setting up testing and production environments.

Platform as a Service

With PaaS, the operating system, middleware, and runtimes are the responsibility of Microsoft. Think of containers as PaaS. The following diagram illustrates the PaaS system:

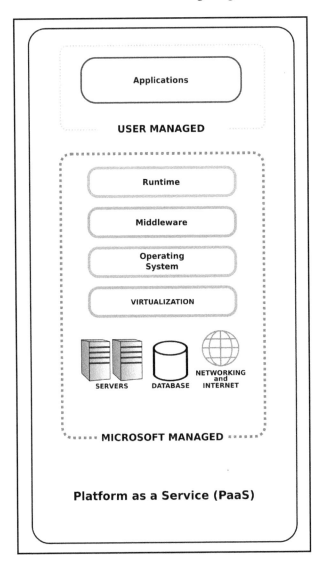

PaaS offers a quick environment in which to deploy applications. The user is responsible only for the applications they install. Typical uses for PaaS are business intelligence and analytics applications.

Software as a Service

With SaaS, the user rents applications from Microsoft. Such applications may include Office 365 and Dynamics CRM Online. The following diagram illustrates a SaaS system:

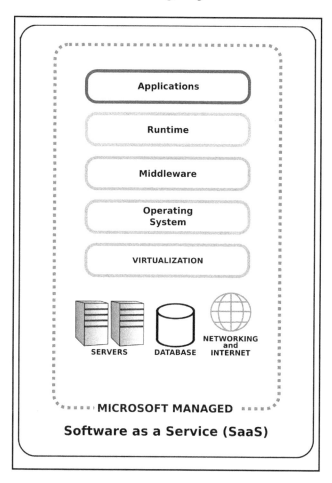

The user has the least amount of control and responsibility for the environment with SaaS.

Functions as a Service

FaaS is the solution for those instances where you want to run functions (usually small pieces of code) in the cloud. FaaS is Azure's answer to serverless computing. Functions are ideal for integrating your locally hosted application with microservices from Azure.

The following diagram shows a typical e-commerce application. As you can see, the website content (HTML) and database are local to the installation of the e-commerce website. Payment processing and email processing are sourced out to microservices. The code for these services is not stored locally but accessed through web service calls. This type of setup allows for a best-in-class approach as the best microservice provider for the task may be implemented into the design:

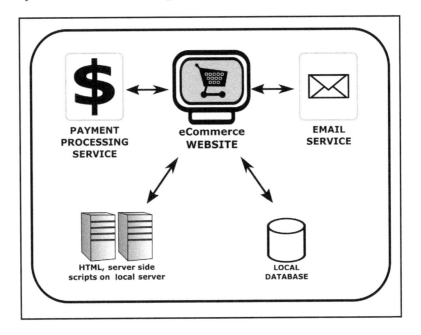

 Microservices is the name given to the development technique of building applications from loosely coupled lightweight services. A good analogy for microservices is the production line model used by automotive makers. Pre-built standard components are assembled to build the car. Microservices are similar in the way that an application is built using pre-built services for such things as payment processing and shipping modules.

Microsoft Azure offers a marketplace where services may be purchased, such as the Mailjet Email Service.

Now that we have an understanding of what Microsoft Azure is, let's set up an Azure account and start getting acquainted with the Azure portal.

Setting up a Microsoft Azure account

Microsoft offers 12 months of popular Azure services free for new accounts. This offer also includes $200 credit for 30 days. To start, go to `http://www.azure.microsoft.com` and click on the **Start free** button.

Walk through the steps to set up a new account. You may need to provide a credit card number for identification purposes. Once you have your Azure account set up, navigate to `http://portal.azure.com` to get to the Azure portal.

Let's take a cursory look at the portal.

Exploring the Azure portal

Upon logging into the portal, you will see a row of buttons and links. The first row on the portal shows buttons that allow us to easily set up Azure services. The **Create a resource** button is always located on the far left. Buttons to the right of it change depending on when they were used, with the most recent one immediately to the right of **Create a new resource**:

The second row displays the recent resources used. As you can see in the following screenshot, an IoT Hub called **HandsOnAzureIoTHub** was last viewed 11 minutes ago. Clicking on the name brings you to another screen where we may modify the resource:

Recent resources			
	NAME	TYPE	LAST VIEWED
	HandsOnAzureIoTHub	IoT Hub	11 min ago

Please note that if you have not created any resources or have deleted all of your resources, the **Recent resources** row will not be displayed.

The third row on the portal allows us to view our Azure subscriptions, the resource groups created, all of the resources created, and the dashboard. We will be creating a new resource and resource group in the tutorial covered in a later section, *A quick tutorial on Azure IoT Hub*. The following screenshot shows the third row:

The tools row on the portal provides resources for learning Azure as well as ways to monitor and control costs. The lessons under the Microsoft Learn resource are excellent and provide a path to be certified in Azure:

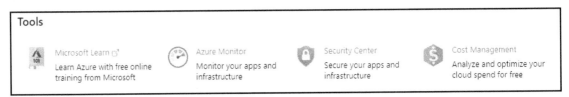

Digging deep into all of the resources of Azure is beyond the scope of this book. We are only concerned with a few Azure resources, such as Azure IoT Hub. Let's take a look at Azure IoT Hub.

What is Azure IoT Hub?

In Chapter 1, *Introduction to Edge Analytics*, we described Azure IoT as a collection of Microsoft Azure cloud services used to build IoT applications. The following screenshot is a list of the cloud services that make up Azure IoT:

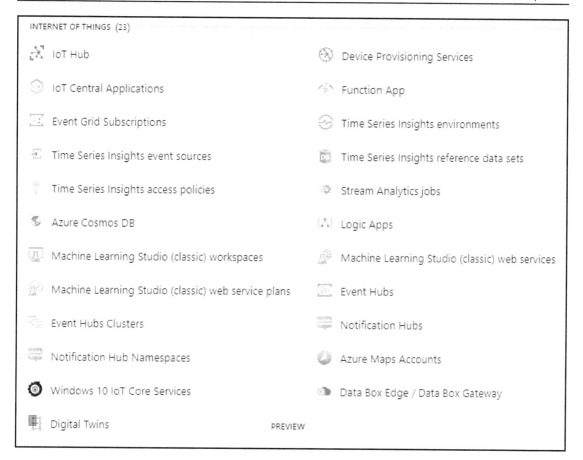

Azure IoT Hub is one of these services. Azure IoT Hub is a managed service hosted in the cloud that allows for two-way communication between an IoT application and its devices. Put another way, Azure IoT Hub is the *hub* for your IoT application. A simple IoT application using only the IoT Hub without the other Azure IoT services is easy to set up and run.

In the following tutorial, we will build such an application.

A quick tutorial on Azure IoT Hub

In this section, we will build a simulated version of a typical IoT application using the Azure IoT Hub. In the following diagram, you can see a temperature sensor connected to the Azure IoT Hub, which is then picked up by a Windows PC:

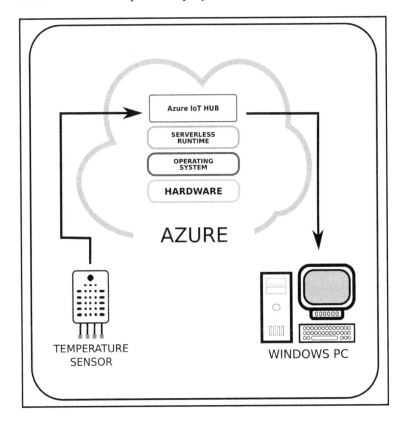

Instead of hooking up an actual temperature sensor, we will simulate it with a Python program. If you do not already have an Azure account/subscription, you will need to sign up and create one.

For this tutorial, you will require the following:

- An Azure account/subscription
- A computer running Python 3.7+
- A Windows computer to run a small utility

Let's get started.

Creating an Azure IoT Hub

To begin, we will create an IoT Hub in Azure. The steps are as follows:

1. Navigate to the home page of the Azure portal (`http://www.portal.azure.com`).
2. Click on the **Create a resource** button.
3. Click on **Internet of Things** and then **IoT Hub**.

You should see a screen that looks like the following:

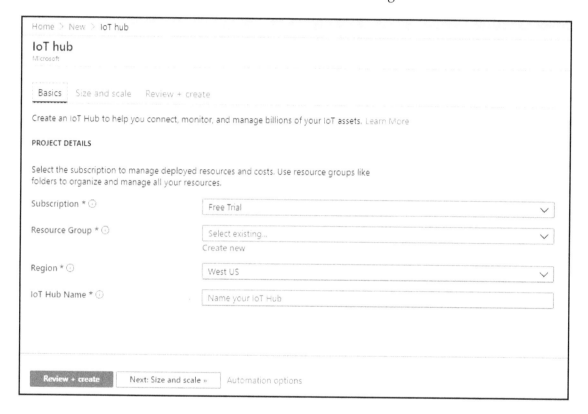

If you have signed up for a free trial, you will see **Free Trial** under the **Subscription** setting. For **Resource Group**, we will create a new one.

4. Click on **Create new** under the second drop-down box.
5. For the name, enter one that relates to the project. For our tutorial, I entered `AzureIoTExample`.
6. Select a **Region** that is close to you. I selected **Central Canada**.
7. Enter a unique name for **IoT Hub Name**. I entered `HandsOnIoTHub`. Your name should be different:

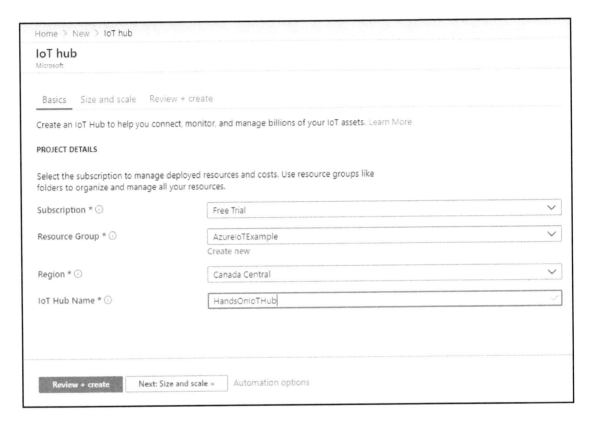

8. Click on the **Next: Size and scale** button to get to the next page.

9. For **Pricing and scale tier**, select **F1: Free tier**. This tier should be sufficient for our purposes:

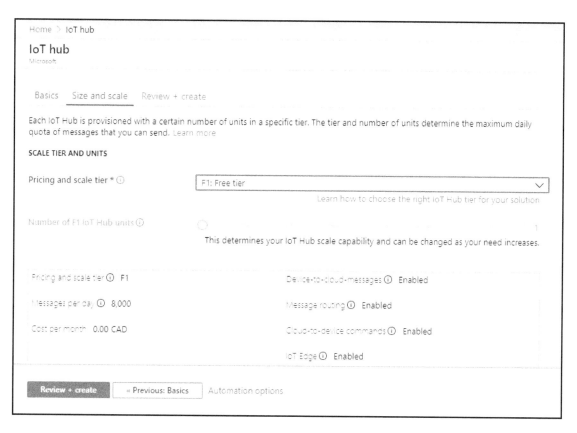

10. Click on **Review + create** to review the configuration.
11. Note how we have a limit of 8,000 messages per day, which is more than what we need for this tutorial. Click on the **Create** button.
12. After a few minutes, you will see a message indicating that the deployment is complete. Click on the **Go to resource** button.
13. To connect to our Azure IoT Hub, we require the connection string. Under **Settings**, click on **Shared access policies**.
14. Under **Policy**, click on **iothubowner**.
15. On the right-hand side, locate **Connection string—primary key**.

16. Click on the **Copy to clipboard** button (two pages icon) to copy the connection string to your clipboard:

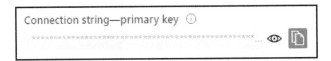

17. Copy the connection string to a text file. We will require the connection string in the next step.

Connecting to Azure IoT Hub with the Device Explorer tool

If you were to explore the documentation on the Azure portal, you will find Azure IoT Hub tutorials that use the Azure Cloud Shell from the portal. Personally, I prefer to use non-portal tools as it demonstrates the *things* part of the *Internet of Things* more accurately. Microsoft built the **Device Explorer** tool for Windows for such a purpose. Let's begin:

1. To install the Device Explorer tool, navigate to `https://github.com/Azure/azure-iot-sdk-csharp/releases/tag/2018-3-13` and locate the `SetupDeviceExplorer.msi` file at the bottom of the page.

2. Download `SetupDeviceExplorer.msi` and install it onto your Windows PC.

3. Once installed, locate the program in your start menu and open it. It will be called **Device Explorer** in your menu and **Device Explorer Twin** once it is loaded.

4. Copy and paste the connection string from *step 17* in the previous section into the **IoT Hub Connection String** box.

5. Click on the **Update** button.

6. An information box will pop up, indicating that the connection settings were updated successfully:

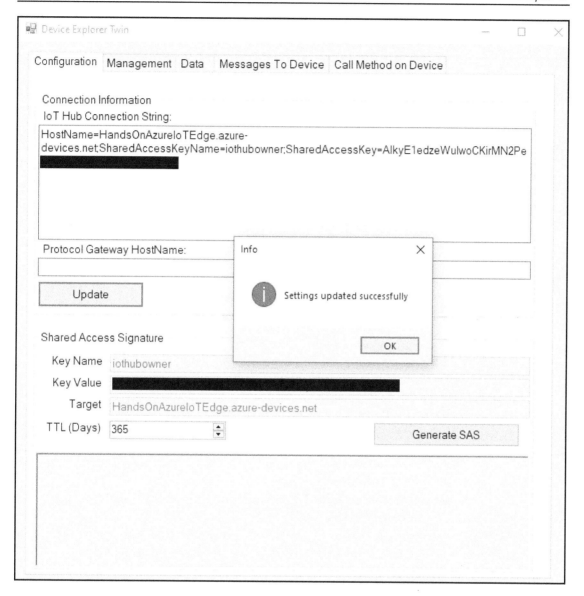

7. Click **OK** to close the information box.
8. We will now create a device to connect to the IoT hub. Select the **Management** tab at the top and click on the **Create** button under **Actions**.

9. Give your device a name. I used the name `PythonIoTDevice`:

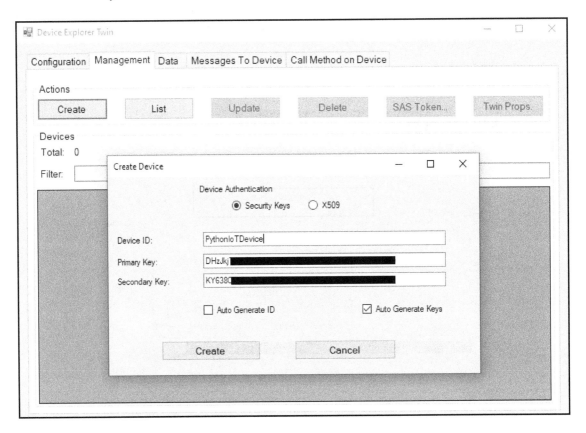

10. Click on the **Create** button.
11. You will see a **Device Connected** dialog upon the successful creation of the device. Click on **Done** to close the dialog.
12. We now need the connection string from this device. In the following table, right-click on the field below the **ConnectionString** heading and select **Copy connection string for selected device(s)**. You may need to move the horizontal scroll bar over to get to the field:

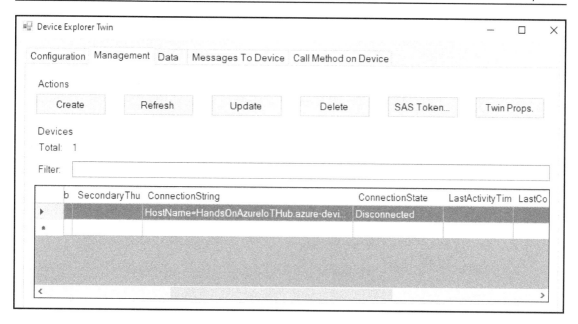

13. Paste the string into a text file. We will require it in the next step when we create a Python client.

Creating simulated sensor data using Python

For our temperature sensor, we will simulate it using a Python program. You may use the same Windows computer running **Device Explorer** or a separate one. You may use your favorite Python development platform or the command line. Please ensure that you are using version 3.7 or higher of Python:

1. Before we can connect to our Azure IoT Hub with Python, we will require the appropriate libraries. Using `pip`, install the Azure IoT Device library with the following command:

```
pip install azure-iot-device
```

2. In your favorite Python editor, create a new Python file and name it `SimulatedDevicePython.py`.

3. Enter the following code into the file and save it:

```python
from azure.iot.device import IoTHubDeviceClient, Message
from time import sleep

CONNECTION_STRING = "[PASTE IN CONNECTION STRING]"
temp = "25"
humidity = "50"
message_text = "{'temperature':'" + temp + "', 'humidity':'" +
humidity + "'}"

def connect_client():
    try:
        client = IoTHubDeviceClient.create_from_connection_string\
                (CONNECTION_STRING)
        return client
     except KeyboardInterrupt:
        print("Stopped!")

def run_simulation(client):
    client = client
    while True:
        message = Message(message_text)
        print("Sending message: {}".format(message))
        client.send_message(message)
        print("Message successfully sent")
        sleep(10)

if __name__ == '__main__':
    print("Started simulated device")
    print("Press Ctrl-C to exit")
    run_simulation(connect_client())
```

4. Paste the connection string in place of [PASTE IN CONNECTION STRING].

5. Run the program in your editor or by using the following command in a Terminal:

```
python SimulatedDevicePython.py
```

6. Return to the **Device Explorer** utility and click on the **Data** tab at the top.

7. Click on the **Monitor** button.

8. You should start receiving data in the **EventHub Data** box:

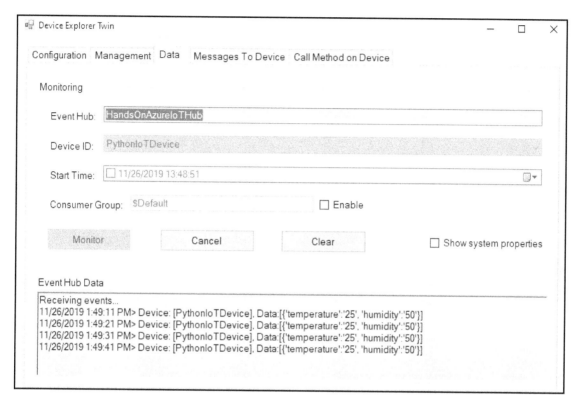

9. To modify the frequency in which simulated temperature data is sent to the IoT hub, change the value for `sleep` in the `run_simulation()` method.

10. To modify the temperature and humidity values, change the values for `temp` and `humidity` in the program.

Now that we can see that the Azure IoT Hub can send messages, let's take a look at what is seen on the Azure portal side.

Viewing usage from the Azure portal

To view IoT Hub usage from the portal, do the following:

1. From the home screen, click on your IoT hub under **Recent resources**.
2. Scroll down to the bottom of the page. You should see charts displaying usage data:

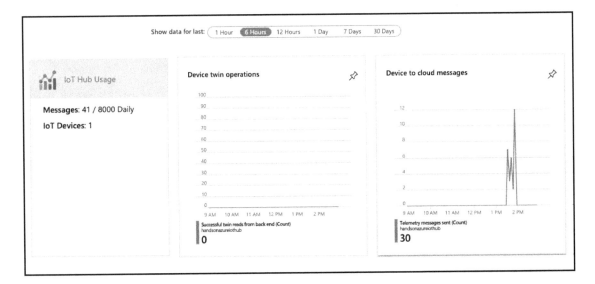

3. The pin icons on the **Device twin operations** and **Device to cloud messages** charts allow for pinning these charts to the Azure Dashboard. Click on the pin for the **Device to cloud messages** chart.
4. To navigate to the **Dashboard**, click on the menu drop-down icon located in the top left of the portal (it looks like three lines).
5. Select **Dashboard**.

You should see the chart we just pinned in the **Dashboard**.

Summary

We started this chapter by discussing the various types of cloud services offered by cloud service providers such as Microsoft. With virtual machines, users have the most control over their cloud computing environment. The IaaS model offers virtual machines where users are responsible for upgrades to the operating system and applications.

Containers provide a quick and stable environment in which to install applications. The PaaS model provides a container environment for such setups. Microsoft also offers SaaS for those only interested in using pre-installed software applications. The FaaS model allows for the construction of microservices for serverless computing application architectures.

After becoming acquainted with the Azure portal, we did a tutorial using the Azure IoT Hub resource. We were able to use the IoT hub to send simulated sensory information from a Python client to a Microsoft created utility designed to set up and monitor IoT devices.

In the next chapter, we will build on what we have learned in this chapter and create an edge computing device.

Questions

Having learned the lessons in this chapter, try answering the following questions on your own:

1. True/False. Microsoft Azure is a cloud computing service.
2. True/False. Power companies are responsible for providing electricity for their customers on demand.
3. What is serverless computing?
4. What is the difference between a virtual machine and a container?
5. True/False. IaaS stands for Internet as a Service.
6. What are microservices?
7. True/False. In a PaaS model, the cloud service provider is responsible for the maintenance of the operating system.
8. What is Azure IoT Hub?
9. True/False. To obtain a client connection string, you must use the Azure Cloud Shell.
10. True/False. The `azure.iot.device` library is required when creating a Python client for Azure IoT Hub.

Further reading

To further your understanding of Microsoft Azure, please refer to the Microsoft Learn center accessed from a link in the Azure portal (`https://docs.microsoft.com/en-us/learn/?WT.mc_id=home_homepage-azureportal-learn`).

5
Using the Raspberry Pi with Azure IoT Edge

The promise of Azure IoT Edge can only be realized when an actual edge device is used. The edge analytics benefits of privacy, latency, and reliability are on full display when we are able to process logic using an edge device, thus the need for a computer that gives us the power to do such, but in a size that allows for easy installation for our applications. The Raspberry Pi is such a computer. In this chapter, we will learn how to utilize the power of the Raspberry Pi as we turn it into an Azure IoT Edge device.

In the previous chapter, we learned a bit about Microsoft Azure and the Azure IoT Hub. This background is essential in understanding Azure IoT Edge. The knowledge gained from the previous chapter will assist us in installing Azure IoT Edge on the Raspberry Pi.

In this chapter, we will look at the following topics:

- Installing Azure IoT Edge on the Raspberry Pi
- Connecting our Raspberry Pi edge device
- Adding a simulated temperature sensor to our edge device

Installing Azure IoT Edge on the Raspberry Pi

In this section, we will install Azure IoT Edge onto our Raspberry Pi. We will use the Raspberry Pi 3B+ model and an older version of the Raspbian operating system.

You will require the following for this section:

- Raspberry Pi Model 3B/3B+
- Micro SD card for the Raspbian operating system
- Raspbian Stretch `.img` file from April 8, 2019
- Windows or Mac computer to create the installation
- Etcher program

Installing the Raspbian Stretch operating system

At the time of writing this book, **Raspbian Buster** is the name given to the latest Raspberry Pi operating system. Buster is based on the Debian 10 Buster, first released on June 24, 2019. Unfortunately for our purposes, Buster broke a few dependencies needed to install Azure IoT Edge. As a result, we are forced to use the version prior to Buster, called **Stretch**. Stretch was first released in 2017 and is based on Debian 9 Stretch.

 As Raspbian is based on the Debian operating system, it takes its version names from Debian as well. A keen observer familiar with Pixar movies would recognize that Debian version names are derived from the characters of the *Toy Story* movie franchise. The first version of Debian to take on these version names was Debian 1.1 Buzz, released in 2006. Raspbian was first released in 2013 and took on the name Wheezy, from Debian 7 Wheezy.

In the following sections, we will install Raspbian Stretch onto our Raspberry Pi.

Downloading and flashing Stretch

The main downloads section from the Raspberry Pi website provides a link to download the latest version of the Raspbian operating system. Since we require an older version, we need to download it from a separate **Uniform Resource Locator** (**URL**). We then need to flash the operating system files onto a micro SD card before installing it onto our Raspberry Pi.

Follow these steps to install Stretch onto a Raspberry Pi 3 Model B/B+:

1. Using a browser on your computer, navigate to `http://downloads.raspberrypi.org/raspbian/images/`.

2. Scroll down to the bottom of the page, and find the `raspbian-2019-04-09` folder. Refer to the following screenshot:

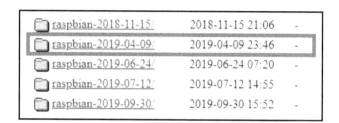

3. This version of Raspbian is the last version of Stretch. Click on the link to get to the index page, as illustrated in the following screenshot:

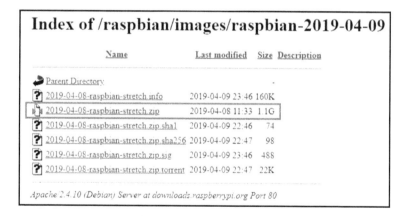

4. The file we are interested in is `2019-04-08-raspbian-stretch.zip`. Click on the link to download it.

5. When the download is complete, you will be presented with a `.zip` file. Unzip the file to view the `2019-04-08-raspbian-stretch.img` file.

6. We now need to flash this onto a micro SD card for use with the Raspberry Pi. A good tool to do this with is Etcher. You can find and download Etcher from the following URL: `http://www.balena.io/etcher`.

7. Once installed, use Etcher to flash Stretch onto the micro SD card. The **user interface** (**UI**) of Etcher is pretty self-explanatory, as can be seen in the following screenshot:

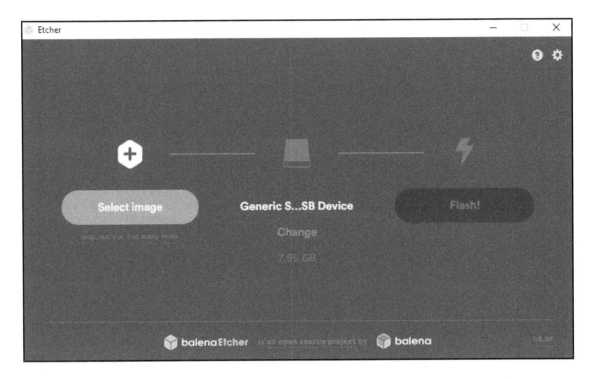

The process will take a few minutes. Be sure to properly eject the micro SD card from your computer once Etcher has finished flashing Stretch. We will now use the micro SD card to set up Stretch on our Raspberry Pi.

Installing Stretch on the Raspberry Pi

As there are many resources outlining how to install Raspbian onto a Raspberry Pi, we will go over this quickly. We are using the older Raspberry Pi 3/3B+ as Stretch will not install on the newer Raspberry Pi 4.

In order to install Raspbian Stretch, do the following:

1. Insert the micro SD card into the bottom of the Raspberry Pi, as demonstrated in the following screenshot:

2. Connect a keyboard, mouse, and monitor to the Raspberry Pi.
3. Power up the Raspberry Pi by plugging in the **Universal Serial Bus** (**USB**) micro power supply.
4. Follow the onscreen instructions for installing Stretch onto the Raspberry Pi. Be sure to update the software when prompted to do so.
5. Restart the Raspberry Pi if prompted.

Now that Raspbian Stretch is installed on our Raspberry Pi, it's time to install Azure IoT Edge.

Installing libraries needed for Azure IoT Edge

To install Azure IoT Edge onto the Raspberry Pi, we first need to install dependencies. We will use the `curl` command to install the required repository information and a **GNU Privacy Guard** (**GPG**) public key before installing the `moby-engine` and `iotedge` libraries with the `apt-get` command.

Installing the repository configuration

In order to install the required container runtime, Moby, the repository on our Raspberry Pi needs to be modified.

To begin, do the following:

1. Open up a Terminal on the Raspberry Pi by clicking on the icon at the top left of the screen (this should be the fourth icon from the left).

2. Type the following code and hit *Enter*:

   ```
   curl
   https://packages.microsoft.com/config/debian/stretch/multiarch/prod
   .list > ./microsoft-prod.list
   ```

3. If you look in the current directory (the default is /home/pi), you will see that a file named microsoft-prod.list was created. We need to copy this file to the appropriate directory. To do this, type in the following command and hit *Enter*:

   ```
   sudo cp ./microsoft-prod.list /etc/apt/sources.list.d/
   ```

4. We now need to install the Microsoft GPG public key. Type the following code and hit *Enter* to download a key:

   ```
   curl https://packages.microsoft.com/keys/microsoft.asc | gpg --
   dearmor > microsoft.gpg
   ```

5. Copy this key to the appropriate location with the following command:

   ```
   sudo cp ./microsoft.gpg /etc/apt/trusted.gpg.d/
   ```

We are now ready to install the container runtime required for Azure IoT Edge.

Installing the Moby container runtime

In Chapter 4, *Working with Microsoft Azure IoT Hub*, we touched on containers. To install Azure IoT Edge onto our Raspberry Pi, we need to install the container runtime, Moby. Before we install this runtime, let's take a brief look at what Moby is.

What is Moby?

If you were to research containers, you would come across various names and acronyms. The name *Moby* has been in use for container technologies since 2017. So, what exactly is Moby?

To put it simply, Moby is an open source framework used to create a container system using libraries of container components, as illustrated in the following diagram:

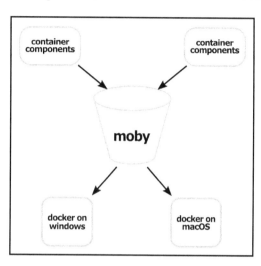

As you may note from the preceding diagram, Moby takes in container components and assembles them to create an operating-system-specific Docker container system. Azure IoT Edge installs itself into a Docker container created by Moby.

Installing Moby onto our Raspberry Pi

To install Moby onto our Raspberry Pi, do the following:

1. Perform an update by typing the following command into a Terminal prompt:

   ```
   sudo apt-get update
   ```

2. Now, install the Moby engine by using the following command:

   ```
   sudo apt-get install moby-engine
   ```

3. Click on *Y* to accept the changes.

You may get an error when trying to install `moby-engine`, whereby a message directs you to install additional packages (`sudo dpkg --configure -a` and `sudo apt --fix-broken install`). Please follow these instructions in order to get past any installation errors you may have.

Now that Moby is installed on our Raspberry Pi, we can proceed to install the Azure IoT Edge security daemon.

Installing the Azure IoT Edge security daemon

The Azure IoT Edge security daemon is used for security standards on the edge device. It is started when the computer boots up, and then continues to start the IoT Edge runtime. With the prerequisite libraries installed, we may install the security daemon by doing the following:

1. In a Terminal window, type the following command to perform an update, and hit *Enter*:

   ```
   sudo apt-get update
   ```

2. Now, type the following command and hit *Enter*:

   ```
   sudo apt-get install iotedge
   ```

3. Type *Y* when prompted to continue.
4. To check on the configuration and network errors, type the following command, and hit *Enter*:

   ```
   sudo iotedge check
   ```

You should see an error regarding the connection string. This error occurs because we haven't actually set up our Raspberry Pi IoT Edge with our Azure account. We will do that in the next section.

Connecting our Raspberry Pi edge device

In the previous section, we installed the necessary libraries for Azure IoT Edge on our Raspberry Pi. In this section, we will go into the Azure portal to create an Azure IoT Edge resource, and then connect it to our Raspberry Pi.

Creating an Azure IoT Edge resource

In order to create an Azure IoT Edge resource, we first have to create an IoT Hub in Azure. In the following sections, we will create an IoT Hub and an IoT Edge resource. We will copy the connection string from the IoT Edge resource and paste it into the Azure IoT Edge configuration on our Raspberry Pi.

Creating an IoT Hub

In `Chapter 4`, *Working with Microsoft Azure IoT Hub,* we created an IoT Hub in Azure. If you still have this IoT Hub from the previous chapter, you may skip over this section.

To create an IoT Hub in Azure, do the following:

1. Log in to your Azure account and navigate to the Azure portal.
2. Click on the **Create a resource** button.
3. In the search box, type in `IoT Hub` and hit *Enter.*
4. You should see a **Create** button used to create an **IoT Hub**, as illustrated in the following screenshot. Click on it:

5. For **Subscription**, use an active subscription.
6. For **Resource Group**, create a new one and give it a name. I've called mine `Ares`.
7. For **Region**, select a region close to you. I've selected **Central Canada**.
8. For **IoT Hub Name**, give it a name. I've called mine `AresHub`.
9. Click on the **Next: Size and scale >>** button to get to the next page.
10. For **Pricing and scale tier**, select **F1: free tier**. This tier should be sufficient for our purposes.
11. Click on the **Review + complete** button to get to the review page.

12. Verify that the **Basics** information is correct and that **F1** is selected under **Pricing and scale tier** (otherwise you may be charged for usage).
13. Click on the **Create** button.
14. You should get a message that your deployment is underway. Wait a few minutes for this to complete. You may push the **Refresh** button if the process seems to stall.
15. When the process is complete, click on the **Go to resource** button to view the new IoT Hub.

We will now attach an Azure IoT Edge resource to our IoT Hub.

Creating an Azure IoT Edge resource

To sync our Azure IoT Edge-enabled Raspberry Pi to the IoT Hub in our Azure account, we need to create an Azure IoT Edge resource on our IoT Hub. This resource will be used to sync our Raspberry Pi with our Azure account. To create the Azure IoT Edge resource, do the following:

1. If you are not already on the IoT Hub page (AresHub) click on it from the home page, under **Recent resources**.
2. In the list on the left, scroll down until you see the **Automatic Device Management** section, as illustrated in the following screenshot:

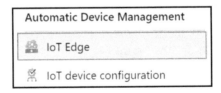

3. Click on **IoT Edge**.
4. You should see a list of IoT Edge devices associated with this IoT Hub (AresHub). The list should be empty. Click on the **Add an IoT Edge device** button, as illustrated in the following screenshot:

5. You will be taken to the **Create a device** page. To create an Azure IoT Edge device resource, enter a name for the **Device ID**. For my example, I've used the name `AresIoTEdge`, as illustrated in the following screenshot:

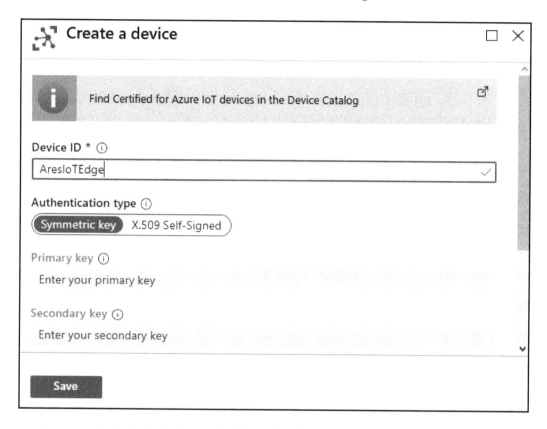

6. Accept all the defaults and click on the **Save** button to create the resource.

7. You should see the new Edge IoT resource in the **IoT Edge devices** list (`AresIoTEdge`). Note that the values for **IoT Edge Module Count**, **Connected Client Count**, and **Deployment Count** are set to **0**, as illustrated in the following screenshot:

Device ID	Runtime Response	IoT Edge Module Cou...	Connected Client Cou...	Deployment Count
AresIoTEdge	N/A	0	0	0

8. Click on the **Device ID** of our newly created resource (`AresIoTEdge`). You will be taken to the details page of the IoT Edge resource. We are interested in the **Primary Connection String**. Scroll down until you can see this field, as illustrated in the following screenshot:

9. Copy the **Primary Connection String** by clicking on the icon that resembles two pieces of paper. Paste the string into a text document. We will be using it in the next section.

To recap, we have used the Microsoft Azure portal to create an IoT Hub. With this IoT Hub, we have created an Azure IoT Edge resource. We then located and copied the **Primary Connection String** from our Azure IoT Edge resource to a text file. In the next section, we will connect the resource to our Raspberry Pi.

Connecting the Raspberry Pi

Now that we have the **Primary Connection String,** we can use it to connect our Raspberry Pi to the Azure IoT Edge resource. To do this, follow these steps:

1. Open up a Terminal on the Raspberry Pi. We are going to use the nano program to modify the configuration of our installed Azure IoT Edge component. Type the following code into the command line, and hit *Enter*:

```
sudo nano /etc/iotedge/config.yaml
```

2. Scroll down to find the **Manual provisioning configuration** section, and locate the device_connection_string variable, as illustrated in the following screenshot:

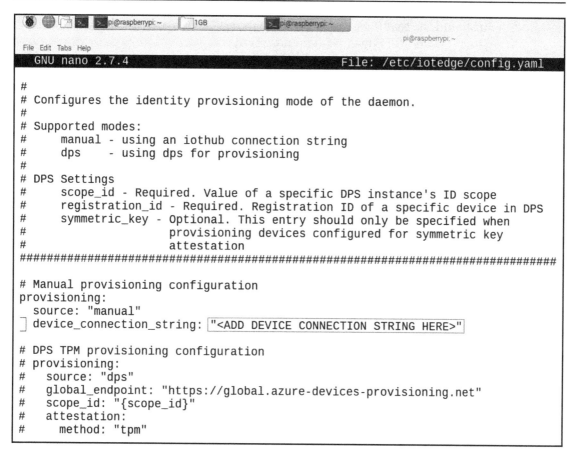

3. Paste in the **Primary Connection String** from the previous step in place of <ADD DEVICE CONNECTION STRING HERE>, and be sure to keep the quotes. You may click on **Edit | Paste** to paste the new connection string.

4. Press *Ctrl* and *X* on your keyboard, and then *Y* and then *Enter* to save the changes.

5. We will now restart the iotedge daemon. Type the following code into the command line, and hit *Enter*:

```
sudo systemctl restart iotedge
```

6. To see the services that are running with our Azure IoT Edge device, we may use the list command. Type the following code into the command line, and hit *Enter*:

```
sudo iotedge list
```

7. You should see that the `edgeAgent` is running. The `edgeAgent` always runs when an Azure IoT Edge installation is set up.

8. To verify that our Azure IoT Edge device is communicating with Azure, navigate back to the Azure portal and go to the home page.

9. Click on our IoT Hub resource (`AresHub`) and scroll down until you see the **IoT Hub Usage** chart. You should see that there is one IoT device shown on the chart, as illustrated in the following screenshot:

10. As there are device twins for every device connected to the IoT Hub, there will be one for the Azure IoT Edge device we just set up. Scroll down a bit more and verify that a device twin was set up, as indicated in the **Device twin operations** chart shown in the following screenshot:

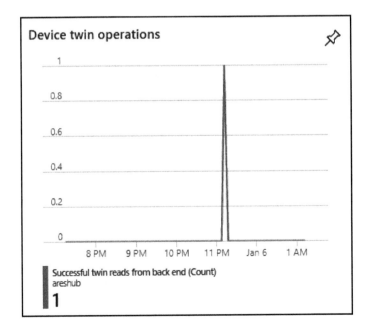

We have successfully turned our Raspberry Pi into an Azure IoT Edge device. In the next section, we will deploy a simulated temperature sensor service to our edge device and view telemetry information using the Microsoft **Device Explorer** application.

Adding a simulated temperature sensor to our edge device

Now that we have created a Raspberry Pi Azure IoT Edge device, let's take it a step further and add a module via the Azure portal. We will use the Simulated Temperature Sensor module for our example.

Adding a module to our edge device

Adding a module to our edge device via the Azure portal is relatively simple. We will start out from the home page of the Azure portal and drill down to our IoT Edge resource, where we will add a module from the Marketplace.

To start, do the following:

1. From the Azure portal home page, click on the IoT Hub resource (AresHub) in the **Recent resources** list.
2. In the list on the left, scroll down to the **Automatic Device Management** section and click on **IoT Edge**.
3. Select the **IoT Edge Devices** resource we created (AresIoTEdge) by clicking on its **Device ID**.
4. Click on the **Set Modules** button at the top left to add a module.
5. Scroll down to the IoT Edge **Modules** list and click on the **Add** drop-down button.

6. Select **Marketplace Module** from the list, as illustrated in the following screenshot:

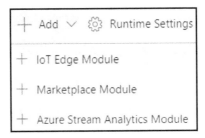

7. Type in `Simulated temperature` in the search and select the **Simulated Temperature Sensor** module, as illustrated in the following screenshot:

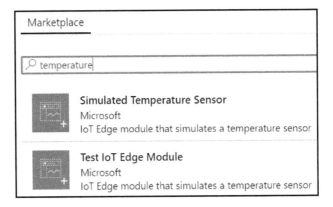

8. Observe from the following screenshot that the new module has been added to the IoT Edge **Modules** list:

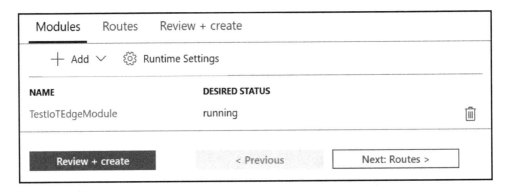

9. Click on the **Review + create** button.

10. Observe that the **Validation passed** message is present. Click on the **Create** button to add the module, as illustrated in the following screenshot:

11. Observe from the following screenshot that the new module has been added to the **Modules** list. Observe as well that the new module, SimulatedTemperatureSensor, has not been reported by the device:

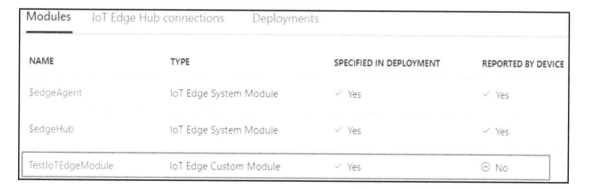

12. We will now restart our Raspberry Pi Azure IoT Edge device. In a Terminal on our Raspberry Pi, type in the following command and hit *Enter*:

```
sudo systemctl restart iotedge
```

13. After a few minutes, use the **Refresh** button in the Azure portal. You should see that the `SimulatedTemperatureSensor` module is now being reported by the Raspberry Pi Azure IoT Edge device, as can be seen in the following screenshot:

Modules	IoT Edge Hub connections	Deployments	
NAME	TYPE	SPECIFIED IN DEPLOYMENT	REPORTED BY DEVICE
$edgeAgent	IoT Edge System Module	✓ Yes	✓ Yes
$edgeHub	IoT Edge System Module	✓ Yes	✓ Yes
SimulatedTemperatureSensor	IoT Edge Custom Module	✓ Yes	✓ Yes

14. To verify that the new module is running on our Raspberry Pi Azure IoT Edge device, type the following command into a Terminal on the Raspberry Pi:

```
sudo iotedge list
```

15. Verify that you can see that the `SimulatedTemperatureSensor` module is running.

16. If we were to view the **IoT Hub Usage** graph from the IoT Hub page, we will see that the number of messages sent is increasing significantly. If left unattended, this number could easily surpass the 8,000-message daily limit. To stop the Azure IoT Edge security daemon and the broadcasting out of simulated data, type the following command into a Terminal on the Raspberry Pi:

```
sudo systemctl stop iotedge
```

We have successfully added a module to our Raspberry Pi Azure IoT Edge device. In order to fully appreciate what our edge device is doing, we will hook up the Microsoft **Device Explorer** tool and view the data coming out from our edge device.

Viewing telemetry data from our edge device

In Chapter 4, *Working with Microsoft Azure IoT Hub*, in the *Connecting to Azure IoT Hub with the Device Explorer tool* section, we installed the **Device Explorer** tool from Microsoft. In this section, we will use this tool to view the telemetry coming from our Raspberry Pi Azure IoT Edge device. We will connect the **Device Explorer** to the IoT Hub and view the output from the edge device. To do this, follow these steps:

1. From the Azure portal home page, click on the IoT Hub resource (AresHub) under the **Recent resources** list.
2. Under the **Settings** list on the left, click on **Shared access policies**.
3. Click on **iothubowner** under the **Policy** list.
4. From the list on the right, scroll down to find the **Connection string—primary key**. Copy the key by clicking on the copy icon (this looks like two pieces of paper), as illustrated in the following screenshot:

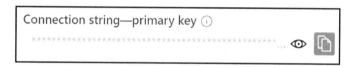

5. Paste the string into the **IoT Hub Connection String** box under the **Connection Information** section of the Microsoft **Device Explorer** tool, as illustrated in the following screenshot:

6. Click on the **Update** button. Observe the **Settings updated successfully** dialog box.

7. Click **OK** to close the dialog.

8. Click on the **Data** tab at the top of the **Device Explorer** tool.

9. Observe that our Azure IoT Edge device is listed beside the **Device ID** (AresIoTEdge). Click on the **Monitor** button, as illustrated in the following screenshot:

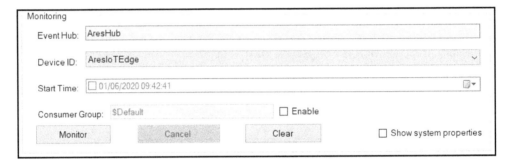

10. Observe that data is received in the **Event Hub Data** box. This data is the simulated temperature, humidity, and pressure data from our Raspberry Pi Azure IoT Edge device, as illustrated in the following screenshot:

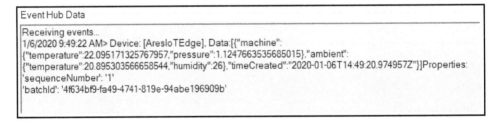

11. If you are not receiving data due to the stoppage of the Azure IoT Edge security daemon in the previous section, start the daemon with sudo systemctl start iotedge, and then restart the daemon with sudo systemctl restart iotedge.

We have successfully added a module to our Raspberry Pi Azure IoT Edge device and are able to monitor telemetry using the Microsoft **Device Explorer** tool.

Summary

As a small yet powerful single-board computer, the Raspberry Pi is a perfect computer to use as an edge device. Using Stretch, a version of the Raspbian operating system, we are able to configure the Raspberry Pi as an Azure IoT Edge device.

In this chapter, we installed the libraries and dependencies needed to turn the Raspberry Pi into an edge device for an Azure IoT Hub. We configured the necessary resources in the Azure portal and used the Microsoft Device Explorer tool to read telemetry data from our Raspberry Pi Azure IoT Edge device.

In the next chapter, we will step away from Microsoft Azure and use the MicroPython programming language for edge analytics.

Questions

Having learned the lessons in this chapter, try answering the following questions on your own:

1. True/False. Debian—and, by extension, Raspbian—releases are named after characters from the *Toy Story* franchise.
2. True/False. As of the writing of this book, Raspbian Buster broke a few dependencies needed to install Azure IoT Edge on the Raspberry Pi.
3. True/False. It is possible to install Raspbian Stretch on the Raspberry Pi 4.
4. What is Moby?
5. What is the command used to install the Azure IoT Edge security daemon?
6. True/False. The Azure IoT Edge resource requires an Azure IoT Hub.
7. True/False. A connection string from an Azure IoT Edge resource is required in order to set up a Raspberry Pi as an Azure IoT Edge device.
8. Where would you view IoT Hub usage?
9. True/False. You may find a test module to test your Azure IoT Edge device from the IoT Edge Module Marketplace.
10. True/False. You may use the Microsoft Device Explorer tool to monitor telemetry from a Raspberry Pi Azure IoT Edge device.

Further reading

To further your understanding of Azure IoT Edge, please refer to the Microsoft Learn Center accessed from a link in the portal.

6
Using MicroPython for Edge Analytics

MicroPython is a subset of Python 3 and was developed as a programming language for microcontrollers. With microcontrollers growing more and more powerful, learning MicroPython is becoming more essential. Imagine having the ability to take your Python knowledge and apply it to the physical world. Imagine building lightweight energy-efficient and powerful edge analytics applications with all of the advantages of using the Python programming language. With MicroPython, you can.

In this chapter, we will explore the MicroPython language, some of the hardware that uses MicroPython, and a MicroPython-based edge analytics application.

The following topics will be covered in this chapter:

- Understanding MicroPython
- Exploring the hardware that runs MicroPython
- Using MicroPython for an edge analytics application

Understanding MicroPython

Launched as a Kickstarter campaign in 2013 by its creator, Damien George, MicroPython is an implementation of the Python 3 language for microcontrollers. MicroPython is run at the *bare metal* layer of the microcontroller, meaning that the language has access to the microcontroller's physical inputs and outputs. This allows developers to use MicroPython to read sensory information such as ambient temperature as well as control motors, relays, and so on. With MicroPython, developers can utilize the power and ease of Python 3 for building things such as robots.

CircuitPython is a version of MicroPython made by Adafruit Industries for use in their brand of microcontrollers. CircuitPython is designed to be easier to use than MicroPython and is geared toward educational use. CircuitPython updates are tied to updates of the MicroPython platform.

To understand more about MicroPython and developing with it, let's compare it to developing with the more traditional Arduino C.

Developing with Arduino C

Arduino consists of a microcontroller board and the Arduino IDE used to program it. The Arduino board comes in various models, including the Arduino Uno, the Arduino Mega, and the Arduino Nano.

The programming language used for Arduino is a version of C. The typical Arduino workflow is shown in the following architectural diagram:

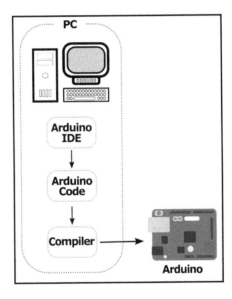

As you can see, a PC is used to write programs that are then compiled and sent to the Arduino board. The following is a typical Arduino program. This example flashes an LED:

```
void setup() {
  pinMode(LED_BUILTIN, OUTPUT);
}
void loop() {
  digitalWrite(LED_BUILTIN, HIGH);
```

```
    delay(1000);
    digitalWrite(LED_BUILTIN, LOW);
    delay(1000);
}
```

All Arduino programs contain a `setup()` and a `loop()` method. In the `setup()` method of our example, we set the built-in LED (an LED on the Arduino board itself) to `OUTPUT` mode. The `setup()` method is run when the Arduino starts up and is run only once.

The `loop()` method is run after `setup()` and runs continuously. In this method, we turn on the LED (`HIGH`) and then turn off the LED (`LOW`) in one-second intervals (`delay(1000)`). The `delay()` function in Arduino C is measured in milliseconds.

Developing with MicroPython

MicroPython is designed to be installed on various microcontrollers. The following is an architectural diagram of MicroPython:

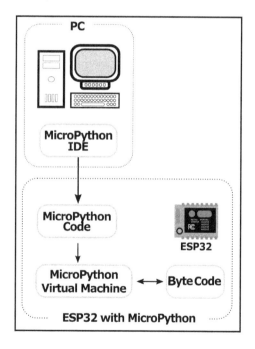

The main difference between Arduino and MicroPython is the place where the code is compiled and run. With Arduino, the code is compiled on the PC before it is uploaded to the Arduino microcontroller. With MicroPython, the code is stored and then executed on the microcontroller.

MicroPython also differs from Arduino in the way code is written. Indents are used in MicroPython instead of curly braces and semi-colons are not required at the end of each line, as they are for C. Here is the MicroPython version of the blinking LED:

```
import pycom
import time

pycom.heartbeat(False)

while True:
    pycom.rgbled(0xFF0000)  # Red
    time.sleep(1)
    pycom.rgbled(0x00FF00)  # Green
    time.sleep(1)
    pycom.rgbled(0x0000FF)  # Blue
    time.sleep(1)
```

This code is written for Pycom boards that have RGB LEDs, such as the WiPy or LoPy boards. The code starts by importing the `pycom` and `time` libraries before turning off the default `heartbeat()` function (flashing blue LED). Unlike Arduino C, there is no default method that runs continuously, so a `while True:` statement is used in its place. The `pycom` library is used to turn on and off the red, green, and blue LEDs in one-second intervals (`time.sleep(1)`).

MicroPython's REPL

The **REPL**, or **Read-Evaluate-Print loop**, is arguably the best feature of MicroPython. The REPL allows developers to use a command line to instantly test code without the need to write and run a program. REPL is an interactive programming environment. Think of it as if you are communicating directly with the computer line by line. You enter a single statement, hit *Enter*, and the statement is executed.

In the following demonstration, we will take a quick look at the REPL with a Windows computer using the uPyCraft IDE and an ESP32.

Installing MicroPython on an ESP32

With a uPyCraft IDE, we can install MicroPython on an ESP32. We can also access REPL and run commands. The installation of uPyCraft is beyond the scope of this book. However, you can find the files and instructions on how to install uPyCraft at `https://github.com/DFRobot/uPyCraft`.

Once you have uPyCraft installed on your computer, perform the following steps to install MicroPython:

1. Connect an ESP32 microcontroller to your computer using the appropriate USB cable (for my tests, I used the Lolin32 v1.0.0 microcontroller).
2. Open up the uPyCraft program and navigate to **Tools | Serial** and select the port that your ESP32 microcontroller is connected to (for my microcontroller, this is **COM7**):

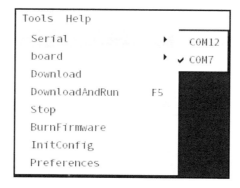

3. Now, select the board by navigating to **Tools | board**. Be sure to select the **esp32** option:

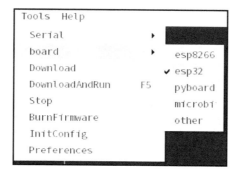

4. To start the burn process, select **Tools** | **BurnFirmware**. You will see the following dialog:

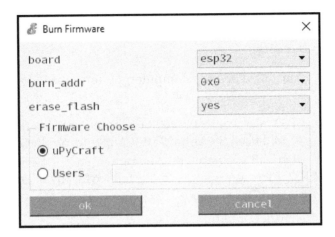

5. Be sure to select **esp32** from the **board** drop-down menu, **0x0** for the **burn_addr,** and **yes** for **erase_flash**. Click on the **ok** button to start the process.

Using REPL with our ESP32

Now that we have MicroPython installed on our microcontroller, let's get familiar with MicroPython's REPL. First, we will connect to our ESP32, and then we will run a few simple lines of code to see that it is working. To start, do the following:

1. To connect the ESP32, click on the **Connect** button from the right panel. The icon resembles a chain, as shown in the following screenshot:

2. After successfully connecting, you should see the REPL prompt in the lower panel (>>>). Let's try typing a command and see what happens. To be consistent with every other first computer language tutorial, type the following and press *Enter*:

```
print('Hello World!')
```

You should see Hello World! print out one line below.

3. You can do basic math with the REPL as well. You do not need to even include the `print` statement. Type the following and press *Enter*:

```
4+7-9+2
```

You should see the answer 4 in the line below.

4. The REPL also provides help with the language. Type the following and hit *Enter*:

```
help()
```

You should see a list of commands, including instructions on how to connect the ESP32 to Wi-Fi.

Now that we understand more about MicroPython, let's take a look at the hardware that runs it.

Exploring the hardware that runs MicroPython

Originally designed for the Pyboard, MicroPython now exists for many other microcontrollers. You may use tools such as uPyCraft (as done in the preceding example), the NODEMCU Firmware Programmer, Thonny, or the popular Python esptool (`pip install esptool`) to flash MicroPython onto a microcontroller.

In this section, we will take a brief look at a few of the microcontrollers that support MicroPython.

Pyboard

The first microcontroller to support MicroPython was the Pyboard. It comes with a Micro SD slot for more memory, a 3-axis accelerometer, analog-to-digital converters, digital-to-analog converters, and four built-in LEDs (red, green, yellow, and blue).

The following is a photograph of the version of Pyboard made by the Chinese company, Sanmuchina. It comes with MicroPython already installed:

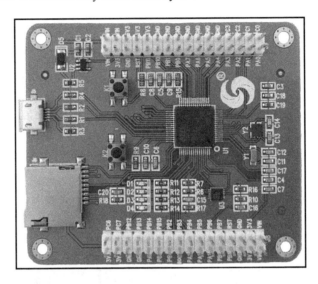

The Pyboard is an excellent tool for getting started with MicroPython. The following code turns each of Pyboard's built-in LEDs on and off:

```
import pyb
leds = [pyb.LED(i) for i in range(1,5)]
n = 0
while True:
  n = (n + 1) % 4
  leds[n].toggle()
  pyb.delay(1000)
```

ESP8266

The ESP8266 is a low-cost, Wi-Fi-enabled microcontroller produced by Espressif Systems out of China. It became very popular after the translation of the Chinese documentation into English in 2014.

Many different models of the ESP8266 exist. The first model, called the ESP01, does not have a USB connection but its small size makes it a perfect component for deployment in small IoT applications.

However, due to the ESP8266's limited resources, it is not a very good microcontroller to use with MicroPython.

ESP32

The successor to the popular ESP8266 is the ESP32. Although slightly more expensive, the ESP32 offers a dual-core processor over the single-core of the ESP8266, support for Bluetooth, and more GPIO pins. The LOLIN32 ESP32 (the following photograph) features a built-in temperature sensor and a hall effect sensor. A hall effect sensor measures magnetic fields. This sensor is used for such things as indicating when doors are closed and measuring the revolutions of a wheel (such as what's in use for a bicycle speedometer):

The following MicroPython code will read and then print data from the hall effect sensor of the LOLIN32:

```
import esp32
import time

while True:
    print(esp32.hall_sensor())
    time.sleep(1)
```

The ESP32 is a low cost, yet powerful, microcontroller. This makes it one of the best platforms for MicroPython development.

Pycom WiPy

Dutch company Pycom aims to create enterprise-level IoT microcontrollers. WiPy (as shown in the following photograph) is their entry-level product and comes with MicroPython pre-installed. WiPy offers an ESP32 chipset and a dual-processor Wi-Fi radio system on a chip:

WiPy also features 4 MB of RAM and the choice of an internal or external Wi-Fi antenna with a range of 1 km. The RGB LED on the WiPy allows the developer to test code quickly.

Pycom LoPy

Pycom's LoPy and, more recently, LoPy 4 offer the same features as the WiPy with the addition of LoRa connectivity:

External antennas may be added for Wi-Fi, Lora, and Sigfox (LoPy 4). It is recommended that an antenna be used for LoRa and Sigfox to avoid damaging the microcontroller.

Similar to the WiPy, LoPy/LoPy 4 has a built-in RGB LED for quick testing of code. LoPy/LoPy 4, like the WiPy, does not come with a built-in USB port and must be programmed through either an extension board, an FTDI adapter, or FTP. Not having a USB connection may seem like a hassle at first; however, this keeps the microcontroller small, lightweight, and ready for production. The use of a USB port is only required in the development stage.

Using MicroPython for an edge analytics application

In `Chapter 3`, *Communications Protocols Used in Edge Analytics*, we described the design of a smart heating system for an ice rink. A Raspberry Pi was used to regulate the temperature based on temperature and camera sensory information.

For this chapter's tutorial, we will modify the design. We will use a Pycom LoPy microcontroller instead of a Raspberry Pi. We will also take out the camera and leave the temperature sensor. We will assume that the rink does not have access to Wi-Fi, so we will use the LoRa communication protocol to send updates to an internet-connected LoRa gateway. From the gateway, we will use the MQTT protocol to update an MQTT broker, which will feed into a Node-RED dashboard.

The following are needed for our design:

- Pycom LoPy or LoPy 4 microcontroller
- FTDI or Pycom expansion board
- Antenna pig tails and antennas
- ESP32 microcontroller with LoRa
- Breadboard and jumpers
- USB cable

The following is a diagram of our design:

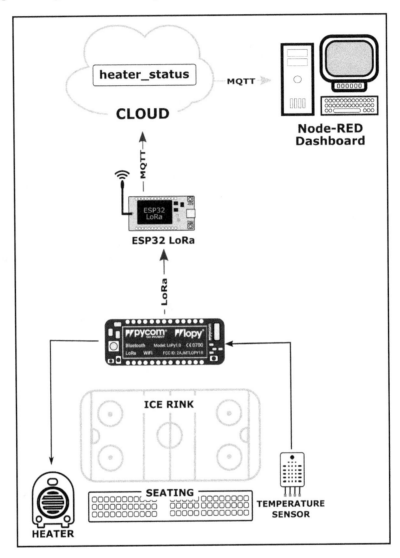

The LoPy/LoPy 4 will act as our edge device. We will simulate the heater using the internal LED and use simulated temperature code for testing. The ESP32 LoRa board will serve as the gateway to our CloudMQTT broker. A Node-RED dashboard will subscribe to a topic from our broker and update a simulated LED.

The logic for the rink heater application is expressed in the following flowchart:

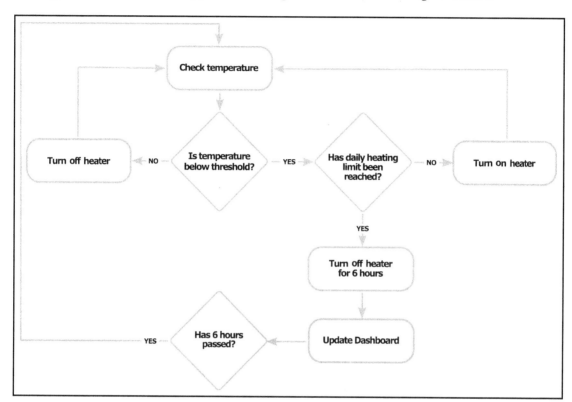

The decisions will be made in the edge device (LoPy/LoPy 4). The code to update the dashboard will be handled by our gateway device (ESP32 LoRa).

We will start by testing out our edge device.

Connecting our edge device

The following are needed for this step:

- Pycom LoPy/LoPy 4 microcontroller
- FTDI adapter or Pycom expansion board
- Antenna pig tail and antenna

- Breadboard and jumpers
- Atom IDE
- USB cable

Let's begin:

1. For those who have purchased a Pycom expansion board, you can use it to connect the LoPy/LoPy 4 to your computer. If not, you can use an FTDI USB to TTL serial adapter. If you have the option of either, choose the FTDI USB to TTL serial adapter as it will be easier to follow the tutorial with this setup. Refer to the following diagram to hook up a LoPy/LoPy 4 to an FTDI adapter. Be sure to use a 3.3V FTDI adapter to avoid damaging the LoPy/LoPy 4:

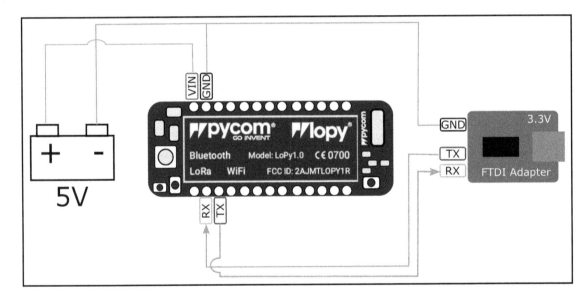

2. To start programming the Pycom LoPy/LoPy 4, we will need an IDE. We will use the Atom IDE with the Pycom extension. In your browser, navigate to www.atom.io and download the latest version of Atom for your operating system and install it. It will automatically open after installation.

3. From the **Welcome** screen, click on the **Install a Package** button and then **Open Installer**.

4. In the **Search Packages** box, type in Pymakr and hit *Enter*, as shown in the following screenshot:

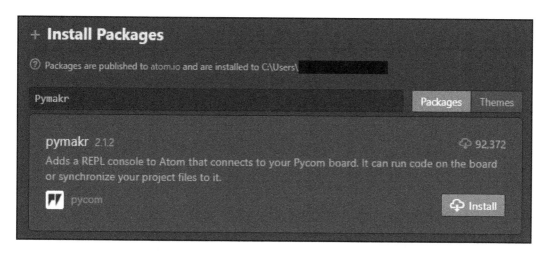

5. Click on the **Install** button to install the Pymakr package.

6. Since we will be writing LoRa code onto our LoPy/LoPy 4, it is a good idea to install the antenna pig tail and antenna to our LoPy/LoPy 4. Gently push the pig tail connector onto the uFL port on the LoPy/LoPy 4 (on the left side below the RGB LED) and screw the antenna into the other end of the pig tail. Be sure to take into account male and female connections when connecting the pig tail to your antenna. You will need to install an antenna that matches the frequency for your region (check for local regulations). Refer to the following photograph:

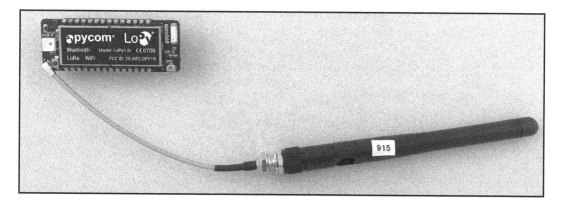

You can also refer to the following chart:

Region	Frequency Band
Europe	863 MHz to 870 MHz
Americas	902 MHz to 928 MHz
Asia	470 MHz to 510 MHz

7. Now connect the LoPy/LoPy 4 to your computer through a USB connection through either the Pycom expansion board or the FTDI USB to TTL serial connection. You should get a message indicating that your LoPy/LoPy 4 has connected in the REPL. If not, then click on the **Connect Device** button and select the port the LoPy/LoPy 4 is connected to.

8. You should see a cursor in the REPL in the bottom panel. Type `help()` and hit *Enter* to verify that the LoPy/LoPy 4 is connected properly:

```
>>> help()
Welcome to MicroPython!
For online docs please visit http://docs.pycom.io

Control commands:
  CTRL-A        -- on a blank line, enter raw REPL mode
  CTRL-B        -- on a blank line, enter normal REPL mode
  CTRL-C        -- interrupt a running program
  CTRL-E        -- on a blank line, enter paste mode
  CTRL-F        -- on a blank line, do a hard reset of the board and enter safe boot
```

9. Now, let's test the REPL using the built-in RGB LED. We will start by importing the `pycom` library. Type the following into the REPL and press *Enter*:

```
import pycom
```

10. Turn off the default blinking blue LED with the following code:

```
pycom.hearbeat(False)
```

11. Turn on the red LED by typing the following code:

```
pycom.rgbled(0xFF0000)
```

You should see the red LED turn on.

Now that we have connected the LoPy/LoPy 4 and ran some basic commands, it's time to wire up the temperature sensor and write the edge device application code.

Writing the edge code

For this step, we will use an external library to read temperature data from a DHT11 temperature sensor. We will then write four of our own classes and upload the code to the LoPy/LoPy 4 microcontroller. The following are required for this step:

- Pycom LoPy/LoPy 4 microcontroller
- DHT11 temperature sensor
- FTDI adapter or Pycom expansion board
- Antenna pig tail and antenna
- Breadboard and jumpers
- Atom IDE with Pycom package
- USB cable

We will start by connecting the temperature sensor before creating the files for the edge device.

Creating the edge device files

Let's begin:

1. The DHT11 temperature sensor is a low-cost, inexpensive, and widely available sensor for measuring temperature and humidity. Using a breadboard, wire up the DHT11 with the LoPy/LoPy 4, as shown in the following diagram:

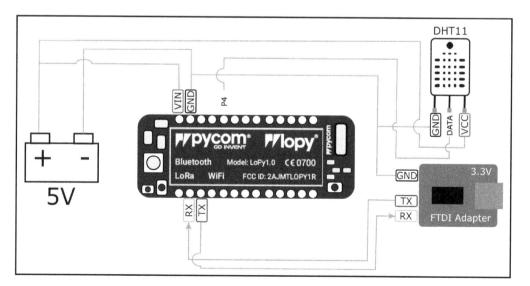

2. We will need to start a new project in Atom for our code. Create a new folder on your computer and give it a descriptive name. I've chosen to call my folder Edge Code. From the Atom **Welcome Guide** screen, click on **Open a Project** and then the **Open a Project** button and open the folder you just created.

3. boot.py() is run whenever the LoPy/LoPy 4 is run. We will require one for our project to set the baud rate. Create a new file by clicking on **File** | **New File** and enter the following:

```
import os
from machine import UART
uart = UART(0, 115200)
os.dupterm(uart)
```

4. Save the file by clicking on **File** | **Save** and entering the name boot.py.

5. We will also need a library to read the DHT11 sensory data. There happens to be one written for Pycom boards that fits in perfectly with our project. Navigate to https://github.com/JurassicPork/DHT_PyCom and download the files. Copy the dth.py file (note the spelling) to the project folder you created. You should see the file under the project name in Atom along with the boot.py file.

6. We need a class for our DHT11 that encapsulates functionality from the dth.py package. In Atom, click on **File** | **New File** and write the following:

```
import pycom
from machine import Pin
from dth import DTH
import uos

class DHT11:
    temp_sensor = DTH(Pin('P4', mode=Pin.OPEN_DRAIN),0)

    def get_temperature(self):
        return self.temp_sensor.read().temperature

    def get_humidity(self):
        return self.temp_sensor.read().humidity

    def get_sim_temperature(self, temp_threshold):
        random_num = uos.urandom(1)[0]
        if(random_num > 100):
            return temp_threshold-1
        else:
            return temp_threshold + 1
```

In the preceding code, we set our DHT11 sensor to pin P4 and then created two methods to return the temperature and humidity data using an import DTH class. We also created a method to return simulated temperatures based on a random number. This will help us with our testing. Save the file with the name DHT11.py.

7. We will need a class to turn our heater on and off. In reality, we will be turning the on-board red LED on and off. Create a new file and insert the following code:

```
import pycom

class Heater:

    def __init__(self):
        pycom.heartbeat(False)

    def on(self):
        pycom.rgbled(0xFF0000)  # Red

    def off(self):
        pycom.rgbled(0x000000)  # Black
```

In the preceding code, we created a class named Heater with two methods, on() and off(). Upon initializing the class (init() method), we turn off the blinking blue heartbeat LED. Save the file as heater.py. You should now have four files listed in the project.

8. Let's test what we have written up to this point. Click on the **Upload project to device** icon (shown in the following screenshot) to load our code onto the LoPy/LoPy 4:

9. We will test the DHT11 class first. In the REPL, type the following code, hitting *Enter* after each line:

```
from dht11 import DHT11
dht11 = DHT11
dht11.get_temperature()
```

You should see a number indicating the temperature of the room.

10. Now, let's test the heater code. In the REPL, type the following lines:

```
from heater import Heater
heater = Heater()
heater.on()
```

You should see the red LED light up on the LoPy/LoPy 4.

11. Type the following in the REPL and the heater should turn off:

```
heater.off()
```

12. Now that our heater and sensory code works, we will need a class to send our LoRa messages. Create a new file called `LoRaMessage.py` and insert the following code:

```
from network import LoRa
import socket

class LoRaMessage:
    def __init__(self):
        try:
            lora = LoRa(mode=LoRa.LORA,
                        frequency=915000000,
                        sf=12,
                        bandwidth=LoRa.BW_125KHZ,
                        coding_rate=LoRa.CODING_4_5)
        except:
            print("ERROR setting up LoRa!")

    def send_message(self, message):
        try:
            s = socket.socket(socket.AF_LORA, socket.SOCK_RAW)
            s.send(message)
        except:
            print("ERROR sending message!")
```

13. The `LoRaMessage` class in this code creates a `LoRa` object called `lora` with a band frequency of `915 MHz`, a spreading factor of 12, a bandwidth of `125 KHz`, and a coding rate of `4.5`. These values are properties of a LoRa signal and will be matched on the receiving end. We need one more file to complete the edge code. Create a new file called `main.py` and insert the following code:

```
from dht11 import DHT11
from heater import Heater
from LoRaMessage import LoRaMessage
from time import sleep
```

```
from utime import time

dht11 = DHT11()
message = LoRaMessage()
heater = Heater()
temp_threshold = 25
max_cycles = 10
num_cycles = 0

while True:
    temperature = dht11.get_temperature()
    #temperature = dht11.get_sim_temperature(temp_threshold)

    if(temperature < temp_threshold):
        num_cycles += 1
        heater.on()
    else:
        heater.off()

    if(num_cycles >= max_cycles):
        heater.off()
        num_cycles = 0
        timer = time() + 21600

        while time() < timer:
            message.send_message("heater_enabled: False")
            print("heater_enabled: False")
            sleep(2)

    message.send_message("heater_enabled: True")
    print("heater_enabled: True")
    sleep(60)
```

Let's take a closer look at the code.

Understanding the edge device code

The main.py file is run after boot.py whenever a MicroPython microcontroller is turned on. In our code, we have a continuous loop that checks the temperature every 60 seconds and compares it to the temperature threshold. If the temperature is too low, the heater is turned on and a cycle counter is incremented. Once the counter reaches the maximum number of cycles, the heater is turned off for 6 hours and a LoRa message is sent out indicating that the heater has been disabled.

The following is a diagram of the `main.py` file:

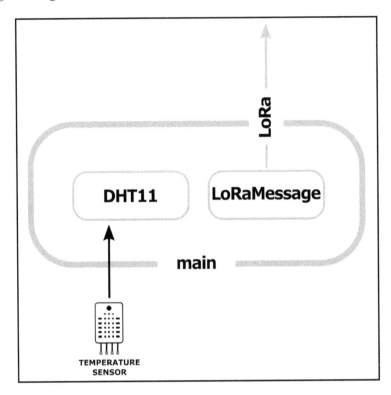

Our code reads the value from a temperature sensor using the `DHT11` class. The `LoRaMessage` class is used to send LoRa messages to the gateway device, indicating whether the heater is enabled or disabled. The following is the code that disables the heater in `main.py`:

```
if(num_cycles >= max_cycles):
        heater.off()
        num_cycles = 0
        timer = time() + 21600

        while time() < timer():
            message.send_message("heater_enabled: False")
            print("heater_enabled: False")
            sleep(2)

        message.send_message("heater_enabled: True")
        print("heater_enabled: True")
```

As we can see in the code, `timer` is set to be 6 hours in the future (`21600`). While time (determined by `time()`) is less than `timer`, we send out a LoRa message every 2 seconds indicating that the heater is currently not enabled (`heater_enable: False`). Once the 6 hours have passed, a LoRa message is sent indicating that the heater is now enabled (`heater_enable: True`).

By using classes in our code, we can abstract details and have `main.py` with a few lines of code, which makes it easier to read and debug. In the next section, we will set up an MQTT broker using the CloudMQTT service.

Creating the MQTT broker

We will use the CloudMQTT service to publish the messages that our heater has been disabled.

Let's get started:

1. In a browser, navigate to `www.cloudmqtt.com` and create an account if you do not already have one. Log in to the account.
2. You should be taken to a page that lists all of your account's instances. Click on the green **Create New Instance** button.
3. Put in a value for **Name**. I chose `Rink Heater`. Select the **Cute Cat (Free)** plan under the **Plan** field:

4. Click on the green **Select Region** button.
5. Select a data center that is close to your location. Click on the green **Review** button.

6. Review your instance before clicking on the green **+ Create New Instance** button.
7. Verify that you see your instance under the **Instances** list:

8. Click on the instance name (**Rink Heater**) to get to the **Instance info** page. Note all of the values. We will be using these values in our code:

 Just after the time of writing, the free Cute Cat plan was not available from CloudMQTT with the message *Out of stock*. You may find this message as well. The lowest cost plan currently available is the Humble Hedgehog, which is priced at $5 per month.

Now that we have the MQTT broker (server), we can now write the gateway code to convert LoRa messages into MQTT messages.

Creating our gateway (ESP32 LoRa)

For our gateway, we will use an ESP32 with LoRa. There are many of these types of boards in the market. They should all pretty much work the same. We will also use a built-in MQTT library to communicate with our MQTT broker.

In the previous section in this chapter, *Installing MicroPython on an ESP32,* we installed MicroPython onto an ESP32. You may refer to that section to install MicroPython on your ESP32 with LoRa or you may use Thonny to do so, as outlined in *step 11* in the following instructions.

Creating the gateway files

We will need to create four files and download a file for the gateway code. We will also download and install Thonny if it is not already installed on your computer:

1. In your browser, navigate to the GitHub location for uPyLoRa (`https://github.com/lemariva/uPyLoRaWAN`) and download the library.

2. If you do not have Thonny installed on your computer, navigate to `www.thonny.org` and download and install it.

3. Create a folder on your computer called `gateway` and copy and paste the `sx127x.py` file from the uPyLoRa library into the folder.

4. In Thonny, under the **This Computer** section, navigate to the `gateway` folder you just created (you may need to select **View** | **Files** to see it):

```
This computer                              ≡  ^
C: \ Users \ sigma \ Desktop \ gateway

     sx127x.py

                                              ∨
```

5. Open up the `sx127x.py` file and scroll down to find the `default_parameters` variable.

6. Change `default_parameters` to match the parameters set in the `lora` variable in the `loramessage.py` file from the *Writing the application edge code* section. For North American LoRa transmission, `default_parameters` appears as follows:

```
default_parameters = {
    'frequency': 915E6,
    'tx_power_level': 2,
    'signal_bandwidth': 125E3,
    'spreading_factor': 12,
```

```
'coding_rate': 4.5,
'preamble_length': 8,
'implicit_header': False,
'sync_word': 0x12,
'enable_CRC': False,
'invert_IQ': False
}
```

7. With MicroPython microcontrollers, the `boot.py` file is the first file that is run when the microcontroller starts. We will need a Wi-Fi connection to the internet for the gateway layer. The `boot.py` file is the perfect place to put the Wi-Fi connection code. Open up Thonny and click on **File** | **New**. Paste in the following code and save the file as `boot.py`. You will need to provide your router's SSID (network name) and password (keep the quotes for both):

```python
def do_connect():
    import network
    sta_if = network.WLAN(network.STA_IF)
    if not sta_if.isconnected():
        print('connecting to network...')
        sta_if.active(True)
        sta_if.connect('<<Your SSID>>', '<<PASSWORD>>')
        while not sta_if.isconnected():
            pass
    print('network config:', sta_if.ifconfig())
do_connect()
```

8. We will need a file to read the LoRa messages from the edge device and a file to send MQTT messages to our CloudMQTT broker. We'll start with the LoRa messages. Create a new file in Thonny called `LoRaMessage.py` and paste in the following code:

```python
from machine import Pin, SPI
from sx127x import SX127x

class LoRaMessage:
    def get_message(self):
        device_pins = {
            'miso':19,
            'mosi':27,
            'ss':18,
            'sck':5,
            'dio_0':26,
            'reset':14
        }

        device_spi = SPI(baudrate = 10000000,
```

```
                    polarity = 0, phase = 0, bits = 8,
                    firstbit = SPI.MSB,
                    sck = Pin(device_pins['sck'], Pin.OUT, \
                            Pin.PULL_DOWN),
                    mosi = Pin(device_pins['mosi'], Pin.OUT, \
                            Pin.PULL_UP),
                    miso = Pin(device_pins['miso'], Pin.IN, \
                            Pin.PULL_UP))

        lora = SX127x(device_spi, pins=device_pins)
        print("Waiting for LoRa message.....")

        while True:
            if(lora.received_packet()):
                payload = lora.read_payload()
                status=str(payload)[18:-1]
                return (status)
```

9. Be sure that the pin numbers in `device_pins` match your microcontroller's LoRa connections. Now, let's create the code for MQTT messages. Create a new file in Thonny called `HeaterStatus.py` and paste in the following code. You will need the values from your CloudMQTT instance:

```
from umqtt.robust import MQTTClient

class HeaterStatus:
    def update(self, status):
        client = MQTTClient(client_id="gateway",
        server="<<CloudMQTT server name>>",
        user="<<CloudMQTT username>>",
        password="<<CloudMQTT password>>",
        port=<<CloudMQTT port number>>)

        client.connect()
        client.publish("heater_enabled",status)
```

10. With the LoRa and MQTT code taken care of, we need a Python file to stitch the code together. Create a new file in Thonny called `main.py` and paste in the following code:

```
from LoRaMessage import LoRaMessage
from HeaterStatus import HeaterStatus

message=LoRaMessage()
heater_status=HeaterStatus()

while True:
```

```
status=message.get_message()
heater_status.update(status)
```

11. We should now have five files in our project. If you haven't already done so, plug the ESP32 microcontroller into a USB port on your computer. In Thonny, select **Run | Select interpreter**. From the drop-down menus, select **MicroPython (ESP32)** and the port in which the ESP32 microcontroller is connected to on your computer. If you have not already flashed MicroPython onto the ESP32, you may do so by clicking on the **Open the dialog for installing or upgrading MicroPython on your device** option:

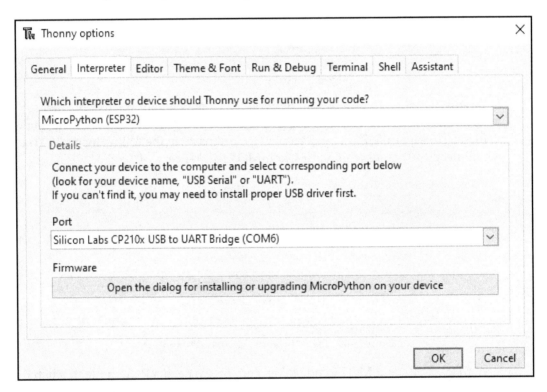

12. Click on **OK**. You should see the cursor of the REPL (>>>) under the shell. Type in the following simple command to verify that the REPL is working properly:

    ```
    print("Testing...")
    ```

    You should see the word Testing... printed below.

13. Now it's time to upload the gateway files to the ESP32. Select all of the files under the **This computer** section, and then right-click and select **Upload to /**:

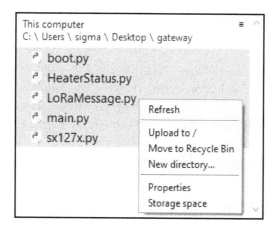

After a few seconds, the files should be seen on the ESP32.

Now that we have the files loaded onto the ESP32 gateway, let's take a look at how it all fits together.

Understanding the gateway code

The following is a diagram of `main.py`:

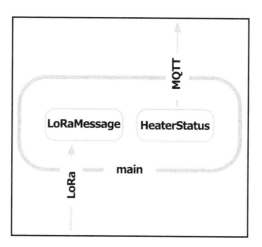

As you can see, `main.py` encapsulates the `LoRaMessage` and `HeaterStatus` classes. The `LoRaMessage` class receives LoRa messages from our edge device and the `HeaterStatus` class converts the LoRa message into an MQTT message to be sent to the cloud.

LoRaMessage

The `LoraMessage` class is built by importing the `Pin`, `SPI`, and `SX127x` classes. The `SPI` (Serial Peripheral Interface) class along with pins physically connected to the onboard LoRa module (on the ESP32 and represented by the `Pin` class) is used to instantiate a LoRa object using the `SX127x` class. After the LoRa object named `lora` is created, an endless `while` loop using `lora` checks for LoRa messages:

```
while True:
    if(lora.received_packet()):
        payload = lora.read_payload()
        status=str(payload)[18:-1]
        return (status)
```

The loop is broken once a message is received. A status of either `True` or `False` is extracted when the payload from the LoRa message is converted into a string and then stripped of the first 18 characters (`[18]:[-1]`). This converts a message of `heater_enabled:` `True` into `True`.

HeaterStatus

The `HeaterStatus` class imports the built-in `MQTTClient` class and uses it to set up a client in the `update()` method:

```
def update(self, status):
    client = MQTTClient(client_id="gateway",
            server="<<CloudMQTT server>>",
            user="<<CloudMQTT username>>",
            password="<<CloudMQTT password>>",
            port=<<CloudMQTT port number>>)

    client.connect()
    client.publish("heater_enabled",status)
```

The `MQTTClient` object, `client`, is created with values from our CloudMQTT account. Its `connect()` method is called and a message is published using the `publish()` method. In this case, a `heater_enabled` message along with the status is passed into the `update()` method.

With the `LoRaMessage` and `HeaterStatus` classes created, it becomes very simple for the `main.py` file to create an outgoing MQTT message from an incoming LoRa message. In the code, a `LoRaMessage` object named `message` is created and the `get_message()` method returns the status of the heater and is stored in a variable called `status`. A `HeaterStatus` object named `heater_status` is created and its `update` method is called by passing in the `status` variable. A continuous loop checks for LoRa messages and sends out the response via the `status` variable:

```
message=LoRaMessage()
heater_status=HeaterStatus()

while True:
    status=message.get_message()
    heater_status.update(status)
```

Creating the dashboard

We create our dashboard using the Node-RED program. Node-RED is a visual programming tool written in JavaScript. To install Node-RED for your operating system of choice, go to `https://nodered.org/docs/getting-started/` and click on the link associated with where you want to install Node-RED.

Let's begin:

1. Before we can use Node-RED to create our dashboard, we need to install the dashboard components. Using the Node-RED Terminal, type in the following command to install the Node-RED dashboard components. You may need to restart Node-RED to see the change:

    npm install node-red-dashboard

2. For our Node-RED program, we will need three components. We will start by dragging the **mqtt** component in the component under the **network** heading to the flow screen.
3. Double-click on the component to see its properties.
4. Click on the pencil icon to the far right of the **Server** label.
5. This is where we add the properties from our CloudMQTT instance. For **Server**, enter the server address, and for **Port**, enter the port number.

6. Click on the **Security** tab and enter the **Username** and **Password** from our CloudMQTT instance. Click on the red **Update** button to save the changes.

7. For **Topic**, enter `heater_enabled`.

8. Click on the **Done** button to close the dialog.

9. Now that we have our data source, we now need to convert it into a format we can use for display. Drag a **function** component to the right of the **mqtt** component in the component. Connect them by dragging a line from the node on the right of the **mqtt** component to the node on the left of the **function** component.

10. Double-click on the **function** component to view its properties. Type in the following code in the **Function** box:

```
if (msg.payload == "True"){
    msg.payload = "green";
}
else {
    msg.payload = "red";
}
return msg;
```

11. This code outputs a color name based on a `True` or `False` value. Click on the **Done** button to close the dialog and save the changes.

12. Drag a **template** component under **dashboard** (not **template** under the **function** section) to the right of the **function** component and attach them using the same method as previously.

13. Double-click on the **template** component and add the following code to the **Template** box:

```
<svg width="100" height="80">
 <circle cx="50" cy="50" r="25"
 style="stroke: none; fill: {{msg.payload}};"/>
</svg>
```

14. Click on the pencil icon to the far right of the **Group** field.

15. Set the **Name** field to `Default` and the **Tab** field to `Home`. Click on the **Update** button at the top-right.

16. Click on the **Done** button.

17. The flow is completed. Verify that you have three components, as shown in the following screenshot:

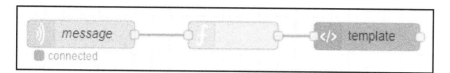

18. It's now time to deploy our application. Click on the red **Deploy** button at the top-right of the screen. You should get a message indicating that it is successfully deployed.

19. To view the dashboard, click on the arrow icon beside the **Theme** tab in the **dashboard** tab:

20. You should see the dashboard open up in a new tab and what appears to be a black dot. This dot represents an LED and is in this state until the dashboard is updated with an MQTT message:

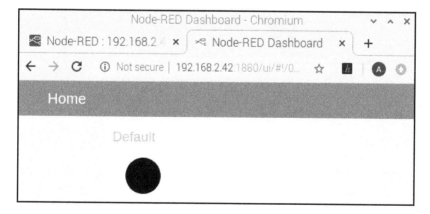

21. Let's test the functionality by updating the color of the LED. Return to the CloudMQTT app and select the instance created. Select **WEBSOCKET UI** from the left panel.

22. In the **Send message** box, enter `heater_enabled` for the **Topic** and `True` for the **Message**. Click on the **Send** button:

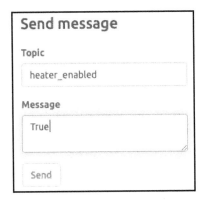

23. Return to the Node-RED dashboard and verify that the LED is green:

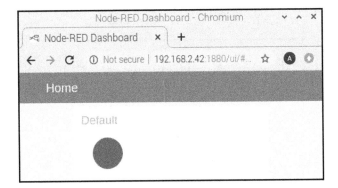

Putting it all together

We now have all of the components for the rink heater built. The next step is to test it:

1. We should already have the gateway code on the ESP32 LoRa board. Ensure that the code is running by restarting the ESP32 LoRa microcontroller.

2. Modify the `main.py` file in the `Edge Code` project in Atom by commenting out the actual temperature sensor code and removing the commenting on the `test()` method:

```
#temperature = dht11.get_temperature()
temperature = dht11.get_sim_temperature(temp_threshold)
```

3. Upload the project code from the `Edge Code` project onto the LoPy/LoPy 4 by clicking on the **Upload project to device** up arrow button.

4. Since the simulated temperature values are random, there is no set time when `num_cycles` reaches `max_cycles` and the LoRa message is sent out. Experiment with the delay values to speed up testing.

5. Load the Node-RED dashboard. The LED should turn to green at first if it is not already green. Verify that when `num_cycles` equals `max_cycles` in the `main.py` file of `Edge Code`, the Node-RED dashboard LED turns to red.

Summary

A lot was covered in this chapter. We started by introducing MicroPython. We compared development with MicroPython to that with Arduino. We also took a look at some of the various microcontrollers that MicroPython is run on.

Our project involved using two separate microcontrollers communicating with each other via the LoRa communication protocol. The project demonstrated a simple edge analytics approach to control the temperature with a heater. The LoRa component of our project emphasized the power of edge analytics in situations where a strong or non-existent Wi-Fi signal exists. The main takeaway from this chapter is how an edge analytics approach may be used to solve a simple problem.

In our next chapter, we will introduce and explore machine learning with edge analytics.

Questions

Having learned the lessons in this chapter, try answering the following questions on your own:

1. True/False. MicroPython started as a Kickstarter campaign.
2. True/False. CircuitPython is a version of MicroPython developed by Adafruit Industries.
3. True/False. Uno, Mega, and Nano are Arduino models.
4. What are the differences between developing with MicroPython as opposed to Arduino?

5. List three programs that may be used to flash MicroPython onto a microcontroller.
6. True/False. The REPL allows a developer to quickly test code by providing a command-line interface.
7. True/False. The first microcontroller to support MicroPython was called Pyboard.
8. Describe how you would hook up a WiPy and LoPy to your computer without the use of a Pycom expansion board.
9. True/False. LoRa works in different frequency bands depending on where you are in the world.
10. True/False. Node-RED is a visual programming tool written in JavaScript.

Further reading

To learn more about using Pycom products such as the LoPy/LoPy 4, visit their documentation site: `https://docs.pycom.io`

Machine Learning and Edge Analytics

7

One of the most exciting fields in technology today is machine learning. As this technology matures and gets into the hands of more and more people, exciting new applications are created, such as a tool for detecting respiratory diseases based on the audio analysis of breathing patterns.

By combining edge analytics with machine learning, the capabilities on the sensory side are enormous. This, combined with the ever-increasing power of microcontrollers and single-board computers, such as the Raspberry Pi, means that the future looks very bright indeed for edge analytics and machine learning.

In this chapter, we will explore the advantages of machine learning at the edge with a Raspberry Pi as we write a program to distinguish between the face of a person and the face of a dog. We will then jump into the exciting new world of **Artificial Intelligence of Things (AIoT)** as we take a small microcontroller and turn it into a QR code decoder tool.

The following topics will be covered:

- Understanding machine learning and how it works with edge analytics
- Using edge intelligence with microcontrollers
- Other offerings of machine learning and Azure IoT Edge

Understanding machine learning and how it works with edge analytics

Machine learning can trace its origins back to 1949 in a book entitled, *The Origins of Behavior*, by Donald Hebb. In his book, Hebb describes concepts that relate to artificial neural networks. Arthur Samuel of IBM coined the phrase **machine learning** in 1952 after inventing a computer program for playing checkers.

For edge analytics, machine learning at the edge brings significant advantages. Picture, if you will, an automated security door application that scans a person's face and performs analysis on the person's voice to determine whether the door should open.

A traditional IoT approach may look like the following:

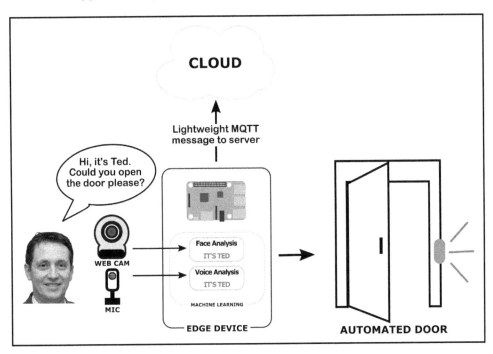

As we can see, a webcam is used to take a picture of Ted's face and a microphone listens to Ted's voice. A copy of the picture and a sound file of Ted's speech is sent to the cloud where machine learning algorithms determine that it is indeed Ted at the door. A signal is sent back down to the edge device and the door is opened.

It is easy to see potential bottlenecks in this design. The following are some of the most likely causes:

- It may take a bit of time to upload the picture and sound file depending on internet traffic at the time.
- Any disruptions to the network may result in Ted waiting at the door for quite some time.
- If the building is located in a remote part of the world, the dependability of the internet connection may be suspect.
- It may be expensive to send this amount of data over the internet.

An edge analytics approach would be to install the machine learning code on the edge device itself, as shown in the following diagram:

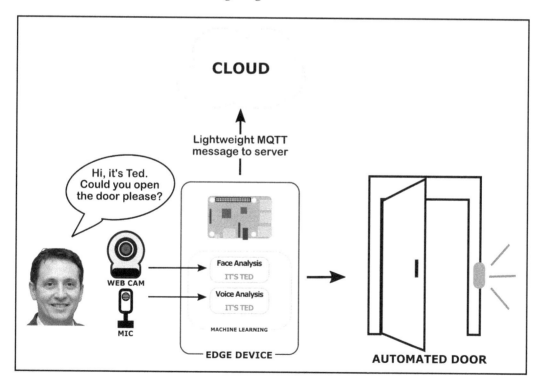

As you can see, there is not a need for a lot of internet bandwidth as the face and voice analysis is done at the edge. The only internet traffic required would be to send a lightweight **Message Queuing Telemetry Transport** (**MQTT**) message to inform that Ted has been granted access. In fact, it doesn't need to even be an MQTT message at all. A LoRa or Sigfox network may be used in place of the internet for remote locations.

Let's take a look at some of the technologies used for machine learning.

Machine learning libraries and tools

There are several technologies and libraries used for machine learning. The following is a list of three such technologies— all of them are open source:

- **TensorFlow**: TensorFlow was created by Google and first released in 2015. It is widely used by many companies and organizations for the automation of tasks and the development of new systems. TensorFlow is a Python-friendly library and may be installed via pip with the `pip install tensorflow` command.
- **PyTorch**: PyTorch was developed by Facebook and released to the public in 2017. It is known for its Pythonic simplicity and efficient memory storage. PyTorch is a competitor to TensorFlow and although PyTorch was released later, studies have shown PyTorch to be overtaking TensorFlow as the most popular machine learning library.
- **OpenCV**: OpenCV stands for the **Open Source Computer Vision** library and is used for manipulating and analyzing images. It was released in 1999 and was initially an Intel research initiative. It is aimed at real-time computer vision.

An example using OpenCV and the Raspberry Pi

Now, let's try an example of machine learning, more specifically, image recognition. In the following diagram, we can see that an alarm sounds off when a human face is detected in a picture. Passing in a picture of a dog does not sound the alarm:

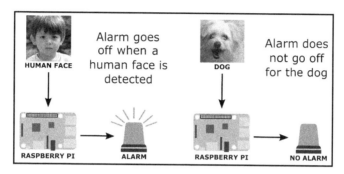

The following is required for our example:

- A Raspberry Pi model 3B or later with Raspbian installed or a Raspbian Desktop computer
- A small breadboard
- A Thonny IDE (should be pre-installed with Raspbian)
- A single-colored LED (preferably red)
- A 3.3K resistor

If you have an old PC that barely runs Windows anymore, you may turn it into a fast Raspbian computer that runs just like a Raspberry Pi. In fact, by connecting a Raspberry Pi Zero computer (without a microSD card) to a USB port, you may then use that Raspberry Pi Zero computer as the GPIO for your Raspbian desktop computer. Visit `https://www.raspberrypi.org/downloads/raspberry-pi-desktop/` to download.

Let's begin!

Running the code

The following are the steps to be performed:

1. Wire the Raspberry Pi with the resistor and LED using GPIO 4 and GND. Be sure to connect GPIO 4 to the positive end of the LED (the longer leg):

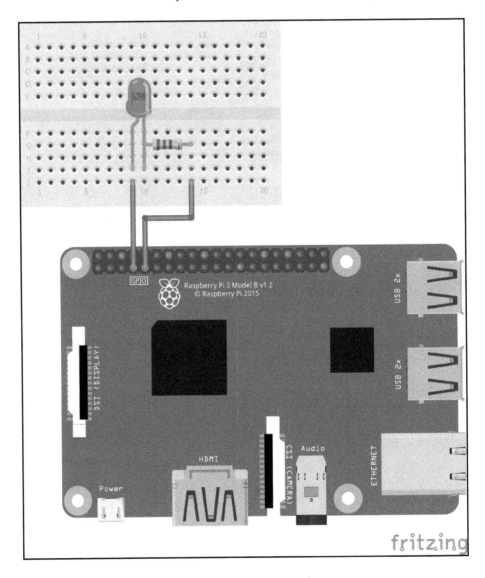

2. The next step is to install the OpenCV library onto our Raspberry Pi. At the time of writing this book, the only way I could get the library installed on my Raspberry Pi was by building it by following the steps from `https://pimylifeup.com/raspberry-pi-opencv/`. For Raspberry Pi Desktop users (refer to the previous tip), installing OpenCV is a simple as using the **Manage packages** tool in Thonny and searching on `opencv-python` and installing it. Please use the method suitable for your setup.

3. We will use Thonny to write our code. Open up Thonny from the main menu in Raspbian and create a new file; name it `face_detect.py` and type in the following code (the picture of the face, the dog, and the cascade file should be in the book's GitHub repository):

```python
import cv2
from gpiozero import LED

image = "face.png"
#image = "dog.png"
cascade_file = "haarcascade_frontalface_default.xml"
alarm = LED(4)

cascade = cv2.CascadeClassifier(cascade_file)
image = cv2.imread(image)
gray = cv2.cvtColor(image, cv2.COLOR_BGR2GRAY)

face = cascade.detectMultiScale(
    gray,
    scaleFactor=1.1,
    minNeighbors=5,
    minSize=(30, 30),
    flags = cv2.CASCADE_SCALE_IMAGE
)

if len(face):
    print("Found a face!")
    alarm.blink()
    for (x, y, w, h) in face:
        cv2.rectangle(image, (x, y), (x+w, y+h), (0, 255, 0), 2)
    cv2.imshow("Face found", image)
else:
    cv2.imshow("Found this", image)
cv2.waitKey(0)
cv2.destroyAllWindows()
alarm.off()
```

4. Run the code by pressing *F5*. Verify that the LED starts blinking and a window pops up with the face surrounded by a green square:

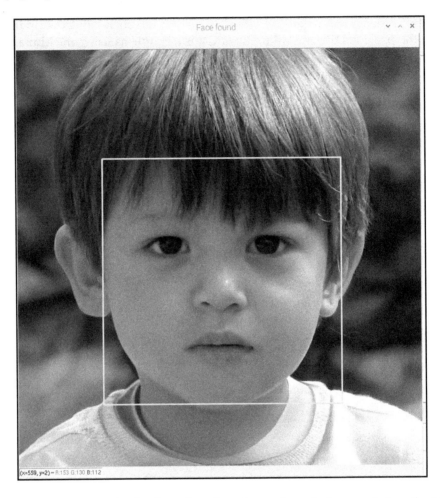

5. Press any key on the keyboard to shut down the window and stop the LED from blinking.
6. Modify the code so that the image of the dog is used instead of the human face by commenting image = "face.png" (that is, adding # at the beginning of the code) and removing the comment (#) from image = "dog.png":

```
#image = "face.png"
image = "dog.png"
```

7. Run the program again and verify that the LED doesn't blink and that the picture of the dog pops up without a green square:

What we have done here is create an alarm when a face is detected. We could easily change the pictures for a video feed from a USB camera and create an alarm whenever a human face is detected by the program. The blinking LED in our example replicates a message call to the outside world. We could change this for an MQTT call to an external server, for example, to be alerted remotely. This example shows the true power of using the edge as the picture is processed in seconds. Significant time would be added to the process if the picture had to be sent to a remote server and that is assuming a strong and quick connection to the internet.

You may be wondering who the person is in the picture of the human face. This person actually never existed. The picture was AI-generated using the website, `https://www.thispersondoesnotexist.com`.

Now that we can see that the Raspberry Pi may be programmed to spot human faces, let's review the code to get a further understanding.

Explaining the code

The magic in our program is performed by the OpenCV library. We start out our code by importing it via cv2. We also import the LED class from gpiozero to control the LED that we will use for the alarm:

```
import cv2
from gpiozero import LED
```

We define our image file as face.png. As there is no directory reference, be sure to have the picture located in the same directory you are running the code from.

To perform image recognition, OpenCV requires a cascade file. This is basically an XML file used to describe what a particular object looks like to the computer. In this case, it is a face in the frontal position, hence the name of the file is haarcascade_frontalface_default.xml.

We then create an alarm object by assigning it to GPIO 4 on the Raspberry Pi:

```
image = "face.png"
#image = "dog.png"
cascade_file = "haarcascade_frontalface_default.xml"
alarm = LED(4)
```

A CascadeClassifier object called cascade is created using cascade_file initialized with the XML file trained for frontal faces. An image object is created from the face.png image. This image object is then used to create a grayscale version of itself and stored in an object called gray. Many operations using OpenCV are performed on grayscale objects as this requires less processing power than operations on colored images:

```
cascade = cv2.CascadeClassifier(cascade_file)
image = cv2.imread(image)
gray = cv2.cvtColor(image, cv2.COLOR_BGR2GRAY)
```

The detectMultiScale() function is used to detect the face in the picture. As mentioned before, the grayscale version of the picture is used and is passed in as the first parameter. The scaleFactor, minNeighbors, minSize, and flags parameters are all set to commonly used values and work well with our picture. scaleFactor may be altered for pictures with more than one face where there may be depth in the picture. minNeighbors and minSize may be adjusted to enhance the performance of the detection algorithm:

```
face = cascade.detectMultiScale(
    gray,
    scaleFactor=1.1,
    minNeighbors=5,
    minSize=(30, 30),
    flags = cv2.CASCADE_SCALE_IMAGE
)
```

To verify whether or not a face or faces are detected, we check the length of the face object. If a face is detected, then we print the message, Found a face!. We then start to blink the LED and iterate through the face object to find the coordinates of the faces (in our case, it is only one). A green—2 pixel-sized—rectangle is drawn around the faces using the coordinates. A dialog entitled **Face found** is created using the imshow() method, with the image and newly drawn rectangle as the content.

If a face is not found, then a dialog named **Found this** is created using the image (without rectangle) as the content:

```
if len(face):
    print("Found a face!")
    alarm.blink()
    for (x, y, w, h) in face:
        cv2.rectangle(image, (x, y), (x+w, y+h), (0, 255, 0), 2)
    cv2.imshow("Face found", image)
else:
    cv2.imshow("Found this", image)
```

In the final lines of the code, we wait for any key to be pressed (cv2.waitKey(0)) before we clean up resources with cv2.destroyAllWindows(). We then turn off the blinking LED with alarm.off():

```
cv2.waitKey(0)
cv2.destroyAllWindows()
alarm.off()
```

With OpenCV, it does not take a lot of code to perform image recognition. We could easily change the objects we are looking for by changing the cascade file. Additional cascade files may be found at `https://github.com/opencv/opencv/tree/master/data/haarcascades`.

Now, we will take a look at microcontrollers as we use one to decipher a QR code.

Using edge intelligence with microcontrollers

As microcontrollers become more powerful, they can process more at the edge. Machine learning-type applications using microcontrollers, particularly in the field of machine vision, are becoming more common. The relatively low cost of these microcontrollers makes it easy to fill up a workshop with many different models and brands.

In this section, we will look at a few of these microcontrollers before we build a QR code reader using the Maix K210 microcontroller.

Exploring the various models of camera-based microcontrollers

The majority of camera-based microcontrollers are based on the ESP32. The two main programming languages for ESP32-based microcontrollers are Arduino C and MicroPython.

The following is a list of three such microcontrollers that can be programmed with either language:

- **ESP32-CAM**: The ESP32-CAM (as shown in the following photograph) is a small-sized, camera-based microcontroller for image recognition applications. It has 520 KB of SRAM, external 4M PSRAM, and microSD card slot for storage:

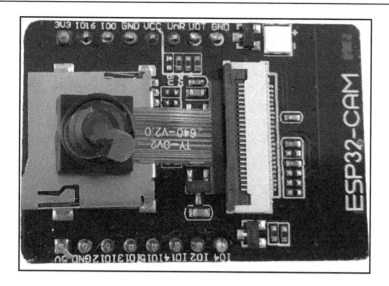

The ESP32-CAM can support the OV2640 and OV7670 cameras and features a built-in flash lamp. With the lack of a USB port, an FTDI USB to TTL serial adapter must be used to program the ESP32 CAM.

- **ESP-EYE**: The ESP-EYE (as shown in the following photograph) is a development board from Espressif for audio processing and image recognition. Unlike many other camera-based microcontrollers, the ESP-EYE features a microphone that may be used for voice command applications:

A built-in USB port allows for the easy setup and programming of the ESP-EYE. With 8 Mbyte PSRAM, 4 Mbyte flash, and a Micro SD card slot, the ESP-EYE is one of the more powerful development boards for edge intelligence applications.

- **Maix K210**: The Maix K210 microcontroller (as shown in the following photograph) is one of the latest AIoT microcontrollers to come out. Made by Chinese company Sipeed, the Maix K210 features a 64-bit dual-core RISC-V CPU with a hardware FPU co-processor. An OV-2640 camera and on-board microphone make this microcontroller perfect for AIoT applications:

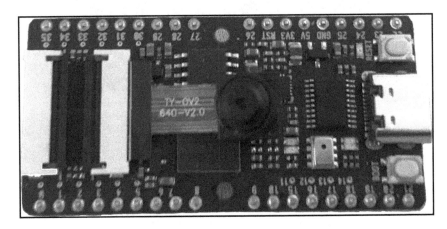

The Maix K210 uses the MaixPy IDE for programming and setup. The MaixPy IDE provides a frame buffer for viewing video from the camera. The Maix K210 comes pre-installed with MicroPython.

Using machine vision to read a QR code

In the following tutorial, we will use the MaixPy IDE and make use of the Maix K210 to view a QR code that we will pass in front of the camera. Our program will decode the QR code and display the value on the screen. To complete the tutorial, the following is needed:

- A Maix K210 microcontroller with camera
- A USB-C to USB type A cable
- A Windows, Mac, or Linux PC for the MaixPy IDE

Let's begin!

Running the code

The following are the steps to be performed:

1. Download and install the latest version of MaixPy IDE for your operating system from `http://dl.sipeed.com/MAIX/MaixPy/ide/`.
2. Connect the Maix K210 microcontroller to a USB port on your computer.
3. Click on the **Connect** button at the bottom left of the screen (it resembles a chain).
4. Select the port the Maix K210 is connected to and click on the **OK** button, as shown in the following screenshot:

5. Click on the **New File** button in the top-left to create a new file and name it `qr-test.py`.
6. Select all of the pre-generated code in the main text area and delete it.
7. Copy and paste the following code in its place:

```
import sensor
import image

sensor.reset()
sensor.set_pixformat(sensor.GRAYSCALE)
sensor.set_framesize(sensor.QVGA)
sensor.set_vflip(1)

while True:
    img = sensor.snapshot()
    res = img.find_qrcodes()

    if len(res) > 0:
        img.draw_string(2,2,res[0].payload(),
                color=(255,255,255),scale=1.5)
```

8. Change the **Histogram** to **Grayscale Color Space** by selecting it from the drop-down arrow on the right, as shown in the following screenshot:

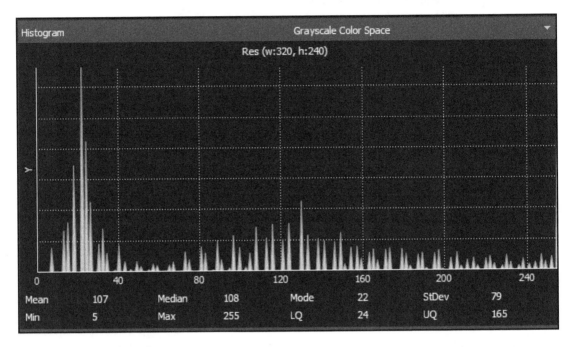

9. Print out onto paper, or load into a phone or tablet, a QR code. You may use the following QR:

10. Run the program by clicking on the **Start** button (the button below the **Connect** button).

11. Place the QR code over the camera using **Frame Buffer** as a reference, as shown in the following screenshot:

12. Verify that you see the text or URL that the QR code represents on the screen.

As you can see, it takes very little code to read a QR code using MicroPython. We could use this code to open a door, for example. It's easy to imagine a hotel chain using regenerated QR codes for room access instead of plastic cards.

Explaining the code

It only takes 12 lines of code to read and display a QR code on screen using MicroPython. The only two libraries we need to import are `sensor` and `image`:

```
import sensor
import image
```

The `sensor` library is used by cameras for taking pictures. We store the resulting object in our code as an image object. Hence, we are required to import the `image` library.

After importing this library, we reset the sensor and then set parameters used for the rest of our code:

```
sensor.reset()
sensor.set_pixformat(sensor.GRAYSCALE)
sensor.set_framesize(sensor.QVGA)
sensor.set_vflip(1)
```

Setting the format to GRAYSCALE as opposed to a color format reduces processing needs. Since QR codes are made with a black and white pattern, a color format would be overkill. The frame size is then set to QVGA or 320 x 240 pixels. To read a QR code, we need to flip the camera, which we do with the set_vflip() method.

An endless loop creates an image object called img from the snapshot() method of the sensor object. The object is then used to create a list of image.qrcode objects, which are stored in res:

```
while True:
    img = sensor.snapshot()
    res = img.find_qrcodes()

    if len(res) > 0:
        img.draw_string(2,2,res[0].payload(),color=(255,255,255),scale=1.5)
```

The while conditional statement checks to see whether there is one or more image.qrcode objects stored in res by using the len method.

Since we know there is only one image.qrcode object (we only exposed one QR code to the camera), we are only interested in the first value in the list. We draw a string onto the screen where the x position is 2 and the y position is 2, and the text is equal to the payload of the first image.qrcode object in res or the actual value of the text that the QR code represents. The color of the text is set to RGB white (255, 255, 255) and the scale of the string (its size) is set to 1.5.

Other offerings of machine learning and Azure IoT Edge

Pushing machine learning to the edge brings all of the benefits of edge computing to a machine learning device. These include increased security, increased reliability, and reduced latency. In this section, we will look at two of Azure's machine learning offerings for IoT Edge, Azure Machine Learning designer, and Azure Custom Vision.

Azure Machine Learning designer

The Azure Machine Learning designer is a visual interface for creating machine learning models. The tool provides an interactive canvas on which the user connects datasets and modules. With the Azure Machine Learning designer, you create pipelines of these connected datasets and modules to publish to a REST endpoint.

You may find an excellent tutorial on predicting automobile prices at `https://docs.microsoft.com/en-us/azure/machine-learning/tutorial-designer-automobile-price-train-score`.

Azure IoT Edge custom vision

Microsoft's custom vision website allows a user to create a Docker file consisting of learned machine learning code. By uploading pictures to the website and classifying them, the machine learning algorithms behind the scenes learn what a particular object is. In the following diagram, you can see that a series of different faces are passed to the custom vision website:

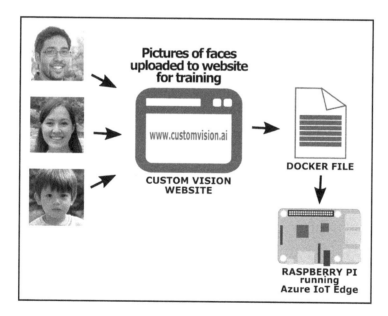

The resulting Docker file may then be deployed to the edge device—in this case, a Raspberry Pi running Azure IoT Edge.

The simplicity of the process means that the user does not have to be a data scientist or programmer to create a learned dataset. An excellent tutorial showing Azure custom vision for IoT Edge may be viewed at `https://github.com/Azure-Samples/Custom-vision-service-iot-edge-raspberry-pi`.

Summary

In this chapter, we looked at the power of combining edge analytics with machine learning. With edge analytics, the latency and reliability of machine learning algorithms are much improved. We looked at how pushing machine learning processing onto the edge improves an application such as an automated security door application, where having a reduced latency is critical.

We then did a practical vision recognition example where our program was able to distinguish a human face from the face of a dog. We looked at the power of the current crop of camera-based microcontrollers by programming it to decode the payload on a QR code. We finished this chapter by taking a brief look at what Microsoft offers for machine learning on the edge.

What you do with the knowledge gained from this chapter is up to you. Maybe you own or know someone who owns a small security firm and may be able to use this knowledge to alert your clients when a person is at the back door. Perhaps you run a small hotel and, as suggested previously, would like to cut down on the cost of keys.

In our next chapter, we will take a lot of what we learned in this chapter and create a smart doorbell using visual recognition.

Questions

Having learned the lessons in this chapter, try answering the following questions on your own:

1. True/False. Machine learning can trace its roots back to the work of Tim Berners-Lee in the 1960s.
2. True/False. TensorFlow was developed and then released to the public in 1991 by Microsoft.

3. True/False. Using the OpenCV library and the appropriate cascade file, we can detect a human face in a picture.
4. What is the name of the Python library we used to flash an LED?
5. List three camera-based microcontroller boards on the market.
6. True/False. The ESP-EYE does not come with a microphone built in.
7. True/False. Scanning a QR code in grayscale reduces the load on the microcontroller's processor.
8. What is the name of the function we apply to the LED to turn it into an alarm?
9. True/False. The URL for Microsoft's custom vision website is `www.customvision.ai`.
10. True/False. The Azure Machine Learning designer is a visual tool for creating machine learning models.

Further reading

We were only able to briefly touch on the amazing machine learning libraries, TensorFlow and PyTorch. Please visit `https://www.tensorflow.org` and `https://pytorch.org`, respectively, for more information.

8
Designing a Smart Doorbell with Visual Recognition

Years ago, the only way to recognize who was knocking at your door, without being too obvious, was through a little peephole near the top of the door. Observant visitors would notice the light disappear from the peephole once a face was pressed up against it on the other side. So, in other words, we really weren't fooling anyone into thinking we weren't home if we decided that the visitor was not worthy of us opening the door. Times have certainly changed. We have the technology now to filter unwanted visitors for us without being detected. Using a camera and visual recognition algorithms on the sensory side, we will design an edge analytics application that alerts us to who is at the door. We won't even have to get up.

In this chapter, we will build a Smart Doorbell using a facial recognition library and a Raspberry Pi. Pictures of potential visitors will be loaded into our program where they will be used to compare to a face seen by a webcam. Upon the webcam detecting a face, an audio message will be heard announcing the identity of the visitor.

In this chapter, we will learn about the following:

- Setting up the environment
- Writing the edge code
- Creating the Node-RED dashboard

Setting up the environment

Our Smart Doorbell is the ultimate edge analytics application by virtue of the heavy processing done on the edge. Our edge device will be a Raspberry Pi. We will use the OpenCV, `face_recognition`, and `paho-mqtt` libraries in Python to write our code.

Before we set up the development environment, let's take a look at a high-level view of the Smart Doorbell application.

Understanding the application

The following is a diagram of the application we will build. For our purposes, we will use a Raspberry Pi Model 4 (4 GB RAM) computer as our edge device. We will require a powerful Raspberry Pi to install the libraries needed for our application as well as for the heavy computation required by the application:

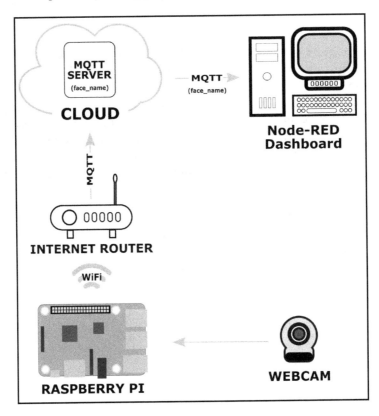

A webcam connected to the Raspberry Pi will provide video frames for analysis. The Raspberry Pi will connect to an internet router via Wi-Fi where an MQTT signal will be published to the cloud. A subscriber on the other end of the MQTT server will receive a message and will display the results on a Node-RED dashboard.

A screen attached to the Raspberry Pi will act as a monitor for the webcam. When a face is detected, the name of the person is displayed on the screen of the Raspberry Pi. Also, a text field on the Node-RED dashboard will display the name and an audio message will play.

If that person is not known, the value *Unknown Person* will be used in its place.

The following diagram is the logic in the form of a flowchart for our Smart Doorbell application:

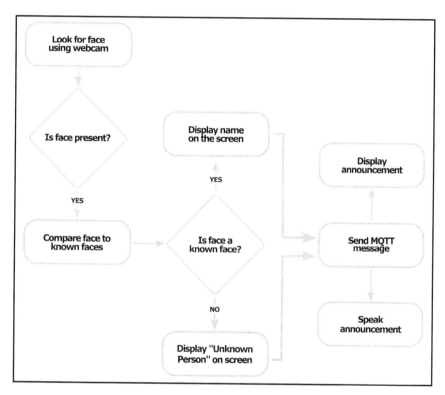

The app starts with input from the webcam. If a face is present, it is compared to a repository of known faces. If a match is found, then the name of the person is displayed on the screen; if not, then the words *Unknown Person* are displayed. An MQTT message with either the name of the person or *Unknown Person* is sent to an MQTT server. A Node-RED dashboard will display the name and announce the visitor using **Text-to-Speech (TTS)**.

Now, let's set up our Raspberry Pi computer for development.

Setting up the development environment

We will use a Python virtual environment for our development. This will allow us a completely separate environment in which to load the external libraries we require for our project. We will need the following for our development environment:

- A Raspberry Pi Model 4 with 4 GB RAM (or a PC with the Raspberry Pi Desktop OS)
- The Raspbian Buster operating system
- A webcam (or Raspberry Pi camera module)
- The Thonny IDE (comes pre-installed with the Raspbian Buster NOOBs operating system)

Let's create the virtual environment.

Creating a Python virtual environment

To create a Python virtual environment using Thonny, do the following:

1. In Thonny, click on **Run | Select Interpreter.**
2. In the drop-down menu, **Which interpreter or device should Thonny use for running your code?**, select **Alternative Python 3 interpreter or virtual environment**.
3. Click on the **Create new virtual environment ...** button:

> Create new virtual environment ...
> (Select existing or create a new empty directory)

4. Navigate to an empty folder and click on **Select Folder**.
5. You should see the **Creating virtual environment** dialog. After a short while, you will see the new virtual environment under the **Known interpreters** field.
6. Click on OK to close the **Thonny options** dialog box.

To verify that we have created a new virtual environment, let's take a look at the limited number of packages in our environment:

1. In Thonny, click on **Tools** | **Manage packages...**.
2. Verify that you see the following two packages (libraries) installed:

Before we can write some code, we will need to install the libraries our code depends on.

Installing the required libraries

We will install the OpenCV library for Python and then the `face_recognition` and `paho-mqtt` libraries. We will use two different methods for installing packages (libraries) in Thonny.

We will start by installing OpenCV using a system shell.

OpenCV for Python

OpenCV is a library for computer vision and machine learning. We will use OpenCV to stream live video from a webcam.

To install OpenCV onto our Raspberry Pi, do the following:

1. In Thonny, click on **Tools | Open system shell....** Verify that you get a Terminal window.

2. Type in `pip install opencv-python`:

```
                              pi@raspberrypi: ~                    ∨  ∧  ✕

 File  Edit  Tabs  Help

************************************************************************
Some Python commands in the PATH of this session:
 - python    -> /home/pi/virtual/bin/python3
 - python3   == /home/pi/virtual/bin/python3
 - python3.7 == /usr/bin/python3.7
 - pip       == /home/pi/virtual/bin/pip
 - pip3      == /home/pi/virtual/bin/pip3
 - pip3.7    == /home/pi/virtual/bin/pip3.7

************************************************************************
pi@raspberrypi:~ $ pip install opencv-python
Looking in indexes: https://pypi.org/simple, https://www.piwheels.org/simple
Collecting opencv-python
  Downloading https://www.piwheels.org/simple/opencv-python/opencv_python-4.1.1.
26-cp37-cp37m-linux_armv7l.whl (10.0MB)
    100% |                                | 10.0MB 28kB/s
Collecting numpy>=1.16.2 (from opencv-python)
  Downloading https://www.piwheels.org/simple/numpy/numpy-1.18.2-cp37-cp37m-linu
x_armv7l.whl (10.4MB)
    100% |                                | 10.4MB 28kB/s
Installing collected packages: numpy, opencv-python
Successfully installed numpy-1.18.2 opencv-python-4.1.1.26
pi@raspberrypi:~ $ 
```

3. Verify that the `opencv-python` and `numpy` libraries install successfully.

If you are having issues installing OpenCV for Python, you may have to build it from scratch. Refer to the instructions at this link: `https://pimylifeup.com/raspberry-pi-opencv/`.

face_recognition

The magic behind the Smart Doorbell application is the `face_recognition` library and the amazing `dlib` ML library it is built on. We will use the package manager to install this library.

To install the `face_recognition` library, do the following:

1. In Thonny, click on **Tools | Manage packages...**
2. Type `face_recognition` in the search box and click on the **Find package from PyPI** button.
3. Click on the **...** box next to the **Install** button at the bottom of the screen:

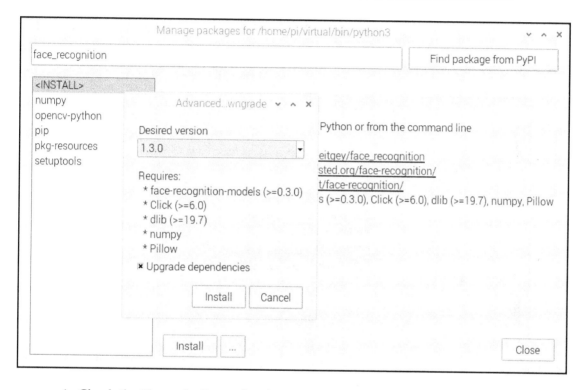

4. Check the **Upgrade dependencies** checkbox and click on the **Install** button below the checkbox.
5. This library and its dependencies will take quite a while to load onto the Raspberry Pi. You may come across errors that will have to be investigated. Verify that you have successfully installed the `face_recognition` library before moving on to the next step.

paho-mqtt

MQTT is the protocol that the Smart Doorbell application uses to communicate to the outside world. For this, we require the `paho-mqtt` library.

To install this library, do the following:

1. In Thonny, click on **Tools** | **Manage packages...**.
2. Type in `paho-mqtt` in the search box and click on the **Find package from PyPI** button.
3. Click on the **...** box next to the **Install** button at the bottom of the screen:

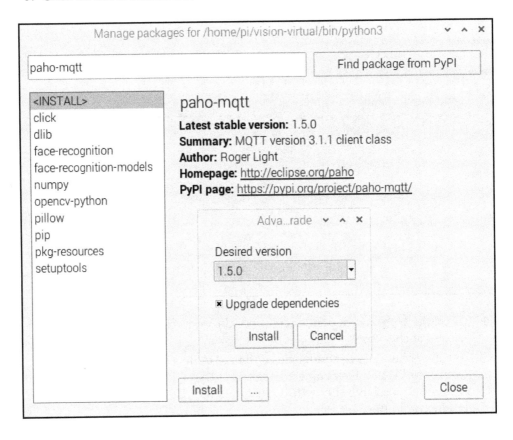

4. Check the **Upgrade dependencies** checkbox and click on the **Install** button below the checkbox.

5. Verify that you are able to successfully install the `paho-mqtt` library before moving on to the next step.

 Personally, I have found that some libraries may produce errors when installed via the system shell, while other libraries produce errors when installed via the package manager. If you find issues with one method of installing libraries in Thonny, you may try the other method—this may resolve them.

Now that we have our development environment set up, let's start writing some code.

Writing the edge code

For the edge component of the Smart Doorbell application, we require two classes and a container script. The following is a diagram of the edge code:

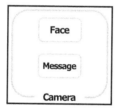

As we can see, `Camera` is the container script that contains the `Face` and `Message` classes.

For our edge code, we will need to create a project folder with a subfolder called `faces`. The `faces` subfolder will store photos of people to train our program with (images available with code are in the GitHub repository).

To do this, follow these steps:

1. In Raspbian, navigate to the `home` directory by clicking on the home folders icon.
2. Right-click to create a new folder called `Smart Doorbell`.
3. Open up the `Smart Doorbell` folder.

4. Right-click to create a new folder called `faces`:

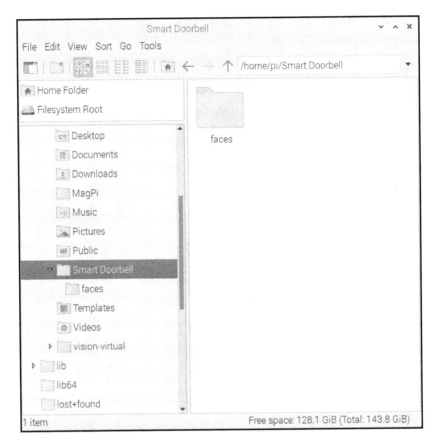

5. In the `faces` folder, copy in photos of people's faces. Make sure that there is only one person per photo or the code will reject that photo.

6. Ensure that the filename of the photo reflects the name of the person. The code will take the name of the person from the filename (the file extension will be stripped off in the code).

Let's start by creating the `Face` class.

Creating the Face class

The Face class is at the heart of the Smart Doorbell application. With the Face class, we can pass in a picture of a person and have the Face class either return the name of that person or state that the person is unknown based on a repository of photos.

The following diagram explains the Face class from a high-level perspective:

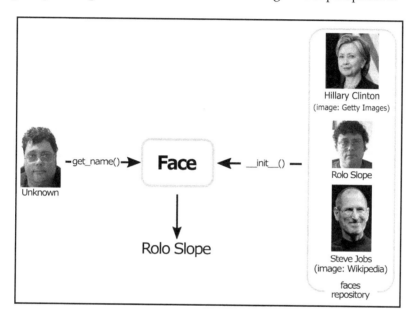

As you can see, Face is instantiated with the faces repository. An unknown face is passed into the get_name() method and compared to faces stored in the faces repository. Of note are the differences between the picture of Rolo Slope in the faces repository and the one used in the get_name() method (it looks like he got a haircut). Despite these differences, our Face object can recognize Rolo Slope.

Let's write the code to create the Face class:

1. In Thonny, create a new Python file in the project folder (Smart Doorbell).
2. Copy the following code and save the file as Face.py:

```
import face_recognition as fr
import os

class Face:
    def __init__(self, faces_dir):
```

```
        self.faces = {}
        for root, dirs, filenames in os.walk(faces_dir):
            for filename in filenames:
                image = fr.load_image_file(faces_dir + "/" + \
                                            filename)
                face_encodings = fr.face_encodings(image)
                if len(face_encodings)==1:
                    self.faces[filename.split(".")[0]] = \
                                            face_encodings
    def get_name(self, source, source_type="file"):
        if source_type=="file":
            image = fr.load_image_file(source)
            unknown_face = fr.face_encodings(image)
        else:
            unknown_face = fr.face_encodings(source)
        if len(unknown_face) != 1:
            return None
        for face_name, face in self.faces.items():
            match = fr.compare_faces([face][0], unknown_face[0])
            if match[0]:
                return face_name
    return "Unknown Person"
```

3. Run the file by clicking on the green **Run current script** button.

4. In the shell, type in the following to import the `Face` class and hit *Enter*:

```
from Face import Face
```

5. To instantiate a `Face` object with the `faces` repository, type the following into the shell and hit *Enter*. Please note that it may take a while for this command to finish:

```
face = Face("faces")
```

6. Now that we have a `Face` object, let's use it to find out the name of `unknown`. Type the following into the shell and hit *Enter:*

```
face.get_name('unknown.jpg')
```

7. Verify that you get the name `Rolo Slope` printed in the shell.

If you are like me, you are amazed that a program to recognize a face can be written with so little code. Let's take a deeper look.

We start with the `import` of the additional libraries we need for the class:

```
import face_recognition as fr
import os
```

After defining the name for the class, we then set up the class initialization method:

```
class Face:
    def __init__(self, faces_dir):
        self.faces = {}
        for root, dirs, filenames in os.walk(faces_dir):
            for filename in filenames:
                image = fr.load_image_file(faces_dir + "/" + filename)
                face_encodings = fr.face_encodings(image)
                if len(face_encodings)==1:
                    self.faces[filename.split(".")[0]] = face_encodings
```

We can see that our initialization function takes in the location of our directory (or folder) where our photos are stored. After defining the `faces` class variable as a dictionary object, we then walk through all of the files in the `faces` folder.

Each file is loaded and stored in a variable called `image`. This variable is then used to create a `face_encodings` object using the `face_recognition` library. A `face_encodings` object represents the faces found in an image or photo. Its length is determined by how many faces it finds. We take advantage of this fact by limiting the `faces` dictionary object to photos with only one face by using the `if` statement, `if len(face_encodings)==1:`. We are not interested in photos with more than one person.

The `get_name()` method takes in a source and compares it to the repository of known faces via the `faces` class variable:

```
def get_name(self, source, source_type="file"):
    if source_type=="file":
        image = fr.load_image_file(source)
        unknown_face = fr.face_encodings(image)
    else:
        unknown_face = fr.face_encodings(source)
    if len(unknown_face) != 1:
        return None
    for face_name, face in self.faces.items():
        match = fr.compare_faces([face][0], unknown_face[0])
        if match[0]:
            return face_name
    return "Unknown Person"
```

The `source_type` parameter in the method's signature allows us to use the `get_name` method for both image files and frames from a webcam. If the source type is a file, then that file is used to create the variable image using the `load_image_file()` method from the `face_recognition` library. The `unknown_face` variable is created from the `face_encodings()` method with either the `image` object or a video frame based on `source_type`. If a face is not found or there is more than one face in the image, then `None` is returned. We are not interested in images or photos where we cannot distinguish one person.

We then cycle through all of the known faces comparing `unknown_face` to known faces stored in the `faces` class variable. If a match is found, then we return the name of the person as a string. If not, then we return the string, `Unknown Person`.

Now, let's take a look at the `Message` class.

Creating the Message class

For sending messages from the edge device to the cloud, we will use the MQTT protocol. We only need to publish to our MQTT server. This makes our code very simple. In `Chapter 6`, *Using MicroPython for Edge Analytics*, we set up a CloudMQTT account. Please refer to this account for the values needed in this step:

1. In Thonny, create a new Python file in the project folder (`Smart Doorbell`).
2. Copy the following code and save the file as `Message.py`:

```
import paho.mqtt.client as mqtt
class Message:
    def update(self, face_name):
        mqttc = mqtt.Client(client_id="smart-doorbell")
        mqttc.username_pw_set('<<username>>', '<<password>>')
        mqttc.connect('<<server name>>', <<port number>>)
        mqttc.publish("face_name", face_name)
```

3. Let's test out the `Message` class. Run the file by clicking on the green **Run current script** button.
4. In the shell, type the following to import `Message`. Hit *Enter*:

```
from Message import Message
```

5. Now, create a new `Message` object with the following:

```
message = Message()
```

6. Now, we will send a test message. Log in to your CloudMQTT account and click on the **WEBSOCKET UI** tab on the left-hand side.

7. Navigate back to Thonny and type the following into the shell:

```
message.update('Rolo Slope')
```

8. Verify that you see the following in the **Received messages** list in CloudMQTT:

The code for the `Message` class is very simple. The `update()` method connects to an MQTT server and publishes `name` using the topic, `face_name`.

Now that we have created the `Face` and `Message` classes, let's turn our attention to the code that stitches the Smart Doorbell application together.

The Camera script

The `Camera` script uses the `Face` class and the `Message` class to identify a person and send out a message respectively. The `Camera` script makes use of the OpenCV library.

To create the script, do the following:

1. In Thonny, create a new Python file in the project folder (`Smart Doorbell`).
2. Copy the following code and save the file as `Camera.py`:

```
import cv2
from Face import Face
from Message import Message
from time import sleep

cap = cv2.VideoCapture(0)

text_position = (10, 30)
font = cv2.FONT_HERSHEY_SIMPLEX
```

```
        scale = 1
        colour = (255, 255, 255)

        face = Face("faces")
        message = Message()

        while(True):
            ret, frame = cap.read()
            name = face.get_name(frame, source_type="video")
            if name:
                cv2.putText(frame, name, text_position, font, scale, \
                            colour)
                message.update(name)
            cv2.imshow('frame',frame)
            if cv2.waitKey(20) & 0xFF == ord('q'):
                break
            sleep(1)
```

3. Run the file by clicking on the green **Run current script** button.
4. You will see a window pop up on your screen showing what the webcam sees. Point the webcam at a person or a picture of a person who has a photo in the `faces` repository.
5. Verify that you get the name of the person displayed on the screen:

6. Verify that you receive a `face_name` message on your CloudMQTT dashboard with the same name.

As with the `Face` class, we can accomplish quite a lot with just a little bit of code. Let's take a look at how this code works.

We start by importing the libraries we need. The OpenCV library is represented by `cv2`:

```
import cv2
from Face import Face
from Message import Message
from time import sleep
```

In the next line, we use the OpenCV library to connect to the webcam. We passed 0 into the `VideoCapture()` method. 0 represents the first camera (or the only camera as there is only one):

```
cap = cv2.VideoCapture(0)
```

We then define the parameters for the onscreen text. The parameters are self-explanatory:

```
text_position = (10, 30)
font = cv2.FONT_HERSHEY_SIMPLEX
scale = 1
colour = (255, 255, 255)
```

Our code then instantiates the `Face` and `Message` objects. The `faces` directory is used as the repository for the `Face` object named `face`:

```
face = Face("faces")
message = Message()
```

The continuous `while` loop that follows creates an object called `frame` using the `read()` method. We then pass `frame` to the `face` object using the `get_name()` method to see whether a face can be found. Of note here is `source_type`, which is equal to `video`. Setting `source_type` to anything other than `file` allows our code to bypass the `load_image_file()` method:

```
while(True):
    ret, frame = cap.read()
    name = face.get_name(frame, source_type="video")
    if name:
        cv2.putText(frame, name, text_position, font, scale, colour)
        message.update(name)
    cv2.imshow('frame',frame)
```

```
        if cv2.waitKey(20) & 0xFF == ord('q'):
            break

    sleep(1)

cap.release()
cv2.destroyAllWindows()
```

If a name is returned, then we use the `putText()` method to print the name on the screen. The parameters passed to the `putText()` method are self-explanatory.

The code then sends out an MQTT message using the `update()` method with the name of the person looking at the webcam (or `Unknown Person` if a match is not found).

The `imshow()` method creates the window that pops up on the screen. For this method, we pass in what we want to display for the window name (`frame`, in this case) and the frame from the stream of the webcam.

The `if` statement that follows (`if cv2.waitKey(20) & 0xFF == ord('q'):`) is used to break out of the loop. The `waitKey()` method waits for 20 ms. The `& 0xFF` performs a bitwise AND operation and in effect masks the value from `waitKey()` so that an 8-bit value is returned. This value is then compared to `q` from the keyboard. Once `q` has been detected, the `while` loop is broken.

The `sleep` function slows down the loop for a second so that the computer does not get overloaded. You may increase this amount as need be.

The final two lines release the camera and close the camera window:

```
cap.release()
cv2.destroyAllWindows()
```

Now that we have the edge code working, it's time to create the Node-RED dashboard.

Creating the Node-RED dashboard

In Chapter 6, *Using MicroPython for Edge* Analytics, we used Node-RED for our dashboard. We will use Node-RED again to create the dashboard for the Smart Doorbell application. Using our dashboard, a message will be displayed indicating who is at the door. A computer voice will also announce the same message. I will be using Node-RED on a Windows 10 machine but you can use whichever OS suits you.

For those that have not installed Node-RED or the dashboard components, please refer to Chapter 6, *Using MicroPython for Edge Analytics*, for instructions on installing these components. The flow diagram for the Smart Doorbell Dashboard will look like the following:

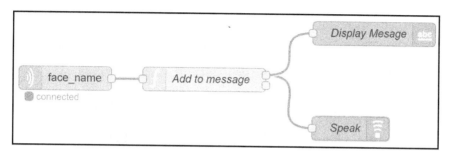

We will start by creating a list of Node-RED components that we will use to build the dashboard.

Adding the components

The Node-RED components we will need for our dashboard are as follows:

- An mqtt in network component
- A function component
- A text dashboard component
- An audio out dashboard component

Let's start with the mqtt in network component.

The mqtt in component

The mqtt in component in Node-RED is used to subscribe to MQTT messages. In Chapter 6, *Using MicroPython for Edge Analytics*, we created an MQTT server using the CloudMQTT website. We will use the settings from this account in this step.

To add an mqtt in component, do the following:

1. You will find the **mqtt in** component under the **network** section on the left. Click and drag the **mqtt in** component onto the canvas.
2. Double-click on the newly created component to get to **Edit mqtt in node**.
3. Click on the pencil icon beside the **Server** textbox.
4. In the **Server** box, copy and paste the server address from your CloudMQTT account.
5. Do the same for the **Port**.
6. Click on the **Security** tab.
7. Fill in the **Username** and **Password** from your CloudMQTT account.
8. Click on the red **Update** button at the top right to return to the original dialog box.
9. In the **Topic** box, put in the value `face_name`. This will set the component to listen for messages with the topic of `face_name`.
10. Click on the red **Done** button to save the changes.

With a connection to the MQTT server in place, it's now time to process the message with a function component.

The function component

The function component is the second component we will add to the dashboard. Function components are used to run JavaScript on the `msg` object. We will use the function component to add text to the message coming from the mqtt in component.

To add a function component, do the following:

1. You will find the **function** component under the **function** section on the left. Click and drag the **function** component onto the canvas.
2. Connect the output of the **mqtt in** component to the input of the **function** component.
3. Double-click on the **function** component to enter **Edit function node**.
4. Set the **Name** field to `Add to Message`.
5. Set the **Outputs** field to `2`.
6. Copy and paste the following code into the **Function** box:

```
msg.payload = msg.payload + ' is at the door!'
return msg;
```

7. Before closing the dialog, confirm that the settings look like the following:

8. Click on the red **Done** button to save the changes.

From the function component, the code diverges in two different directions. In one direction is a simple textbox displaying the name of the visitor. The other is an audio output of the same message.

We will configure the text component first.

The text dashboard component

For the Smart Doorbell dashboard, we will use the text dashboard component to display the output from the function component.

To add a text dashboard component to the dashboard, do the following:

1. You will find the **text** dashboard component under the **dashboard** section on the left. Click and drag the **text** dashboard component onto the canvas.
2. Connect the output of the **function** component to the input of the **text** dashboard component.

3. Double-click on the **text** dashboard component to enter the **Edit text node** dialog box.

4. Fill out the fields as shown in the following screenshot:

5. You may have to create a new **Group** using the pencil icon.

With the text dashboard component in place, all that remains is adding the audio out dashboard component.

The audio out component

We use the **audio out** dashboard component to provide **Text-to-Speech** (**TTS**) functionality to the Smart Doorbell application.

To add the **audio out** dashboard component, do the following:

1. You will find the **audio out** dashboard component under the **dashboard** section on the left. Click and drag the **audio out** dashboard component onto the canvas.
2. Connect the output of the **function** component to the input of the **audio out** dashboard component.
3. Double-click on the **audio out** dashboard component to enter the **Edit audio out node** dialog box.
4. Fill out the fields as shown in the following screenshot:

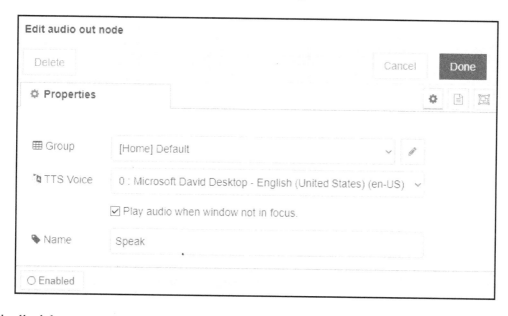

With all of the components added, it's time to run the Smart Doorbell application.

Running the application

We are now ready to run the Smart Doorbell application. We will start by deploying and displaying the Node-RED configuration. After that, we will use Thonny to run `Camera.py`. A recognizable face put in front of the webcam should result in an audio- and text-based announcement of the name of that person.

Let's begin:

1. In Node-RED, click on the red **Deploy** button at the top right.
2. Launch the dashboard by clicking on the launch icon (highlighted with an arrow):

3. In Thonny, open up the `Camera.py` program and run it.
4. Point the webcam at a person or a picture of a person where a photo representing of them is present in the `faces` folder. In my case, I am using a picture of Rolo Slope from my cell phone.
5. Verify that you see the following on the Node-RED dashboard:

6. Verify that you hear the same message.

Congratulations, you have just built and run the Smart Doorbell application!

Summary

In this chapter, we created a Smart Doorbell application that will announce who is at the door once they are picked up by a webcam. By sticking to an object-oriented approach, we were able to organize our edge code into three separate components, the `Face` class, the `Message` class, and the `Camera` script. At the heart of the Smart Doorbell application is the `Face` class. Using the object-oriented approach, we were able to write the code and test the functionality of this class quickly. We were also able to build and test the `Message` class the same way.

In the construction of our edge code, we were introduced to the OpenCV and `face_recognition` libraries. Having these libraries made our task so much easier as they did the majority of the heavy lifting for us. The `paho.mqtt` library made it very easy to connect to the outside world through the use of the MQTT protocol.

An MQTT server provided an easy way to connect our edge code to a Node-RED dashboard. The online service, CloudMQTT, was used for this. The topic our Node-RED dashboard subscribed to gave us a lightweight message that was easy to utilize in our dashboard. Future improvements could be a shared photo repository between the Node-RED dashboard and the edge code so that a picture of the person at the door could be displayed on the screen of the Node-RED dashboard. The Smart Doorbell application marks the end of the projects in this book. I hope that this application instilled in you the power of taking an edge analytics approach to building applications.

In the next chapter, we will look at security and privacy in edge analytics.

Questions

Having learned the lessons in this chapter, try answering the following questions on your own:

1. True/False. The Smart Doorbell application ignores a face it doesn't recognize.
2. True/False. Upon setting up a Python virtual environment, there are only two libraries available.
3. True/False. OpenCV is a library for computer vision.
4. What is the name of the Python library we used to recognize a face?
5. What are the names of the two custom classes used in the `Camera` script?

6. True/False. We use the `paho-mqtt` library to publish MQTT messages.
7. True/False. The `Face` class is instantiated with the location of a folder containing photos of faces.
8. True/False. When the Smart Doorbell application recognizes a face, it displays the name of that person on the screen.
9. True/False. We use the dashboard component, **mqtt out**, to subscribe to the external MQTT server.
10. True/False. Text-to-speech functionality exists in Node-RED.

Further reading

We only touched a bit on the OpenCV and `face_recognition` libraries in this chapter. For further information on these amazing libraries, please visit `https://opencv.org/` and `https://github.com/ageitgey/face_recognition`.

Section 3: The Road Ahead 3

In this section, we will look at security and privacy through the lens of edge analytics. We will then summarize what we have learned in the book and look ahead to the future of this exciting technology.

This section comprises the following chapters:

Security and Privacy in an Edge Analytics World

9

When deploying an application to the internet, the risks posed by cyber criminals should be taken very seriously. Internet-enabled devices, including edge computers, are prone to cyber attacks, where they may be used to shut down websites or cause havoc on the internet—not to mention the destruction that cyber attacks can cause to our networked applications.

In this chapter, we will cover security—and, in turn, privacy—when it comes to our edge analytics applications.

The following topics will be covered in this chapter:

- An overview of the Internet-of-Things security
- Types of attacks against our edge analytics applications
- Protecting our edge analytics applications
- Monitoring and auditing our edge analytics applications

An overview of the Internet-of-Things security

Starting in September 2016, the Mirai botnet launched a **distributed denial of service** (**DDoS**) attack using the **Internet of Things** (**IoT**) devices on some of the biggest websites in the world, including Reddit, Airbnb, and Netflix. Flooding the DNS provider of these websites with more than 1 TB of data per second from captured devices, the cyber attack was one of the biggest DDoS attacks ever recorded.

So, what exactly is a DDoS attack and how are IoT devices involved? The following diagram shows what a DDoS attack with IoT devices might look like:

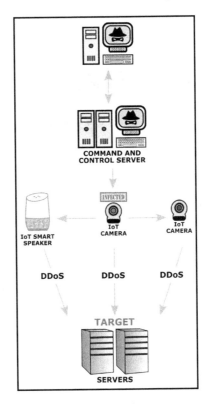

DDoS is an attack on a website that overwhelms it with excessive traffic, causing the website to fail. This type of attack is beneficial to the website's competitors. In the case of the Mirai botnet, the attack was designed by students interested in disabling competing Minecraft servers. The code for the attack was released on the internet to give the creators plausible deniability. However, confessions were made in December 2016 and the main creator was sentenced to 6 months of home confinement and was fined $8.6 million.

What was so significant about the Mirai botnet attack was that it was the first attack to be carried out using IoT devices. At one point, over 600,000 IoT devices, including smart cameras and routers, were used to carry out the attack.

From the preceding diagram, we can see that a command and control server starts the process by infecting an IoT device through the use of malware, which in turn infects other IoT devices. The IoT devices are then used as a distributed network to target an internet service provider with an overwhelming amount of traffic.

So, why target IoT devices for cyber crimes? It turns out that many deployed IoT devices contain default usernames and passwords, as the owners never bothered to change them. To make things worse, some IoT devices actually had hardwired usernames and passwords. Using a list of common values, the Mirai botnet was able to build up its network of compromised devices quickly.

As we can see, security and privacy are very important concepts with regards to IoT devices and, in our case, edge analytics architectures. In the next section, we will look at the types of attacks we may experience on our edge analytics applications.

Types of attacks against our edge analytics applications

By its very nature, an edge analytics application is more secure than a pure IoT application. This is due to the fact that we limit the amount of information that is transmitted over the internet. However, there are still security concerns we must take into account.

The following are three examples of these concerns.

Vulnerability issues

Vulnerabilities in our internet-facing interfaces may be exploited by cyber criminals. These vulnerabilities include using default passwords and out-of-date software updates. In the following diagram, we can see the vulnerabilities of the internet-facing interfaces of the smart doorbell application we built in the previous chapter:

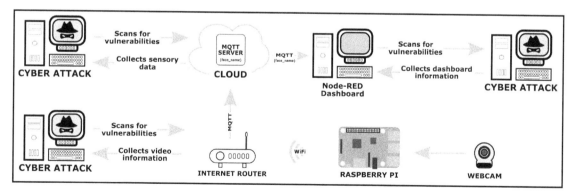

The biggest threat is an attack on an application's internet router. Through the internet router, a cyber criminal can gain access to a repository of photos of people that the application recognizes. This creates a privacy breach as this information could be used for nefarious reasons, possibly without the knowledge of the people in the photo. Also, a breach of the internet router could allow a cyber criminal access to the webcam, where they may be able to spy on the user and their visitors with their own camera.

An attack on an MQTT server exposes a cyber criminal to the messages that an application sends over the internet. These messages may contain information that is of little concern, depending on what they represent, or they may present a huge security threat. Imagine an application that sends warning information messages from a sensor in a factory. If a cyber criminal were to intercept that message and manipulate it, there could be significant damage and perhaps even deadly consequences.

Intercepting messages that are sent to the dashboard of an application is also a threat. Similar to the way intercepted messages to an MQTT server poses a threat, the same threat exists when messages to the dashboard are intercepted.

Sniffing

Exposing vulnerabilities in our internet router gives a cyber criminal the opportunity to set up a sniffer that sits between our router and edge device. The following diagram is an illustration of sniffing in a network:

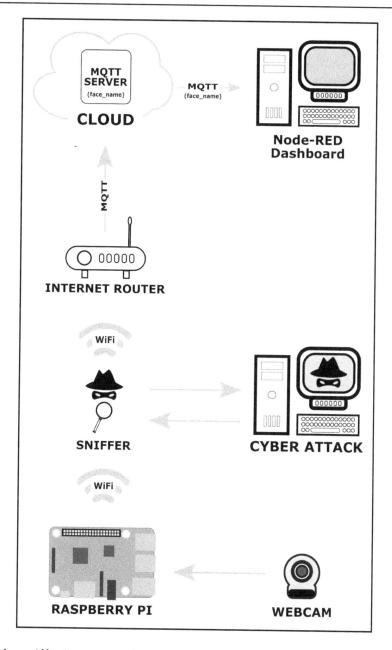

In this setup, the sniffer interrupts the network at a place that gives them direct access to messages before they are sent out over the internet.

Spoofing

Spoofing is similar to sniffing in the way that a cyber criminal gains access to our applications from behind the internet router. In spoofing, a disguised device pretends to be a legitimate device in our application. The following diagram illustrates spoofing in a network:

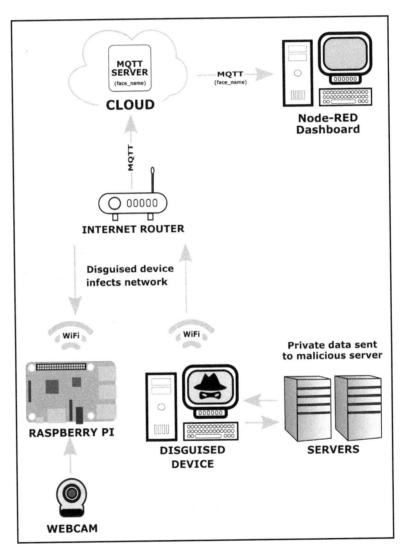

Once the disguised device has established this access, it may then infect other devices with malware and also use them in DDoS attacks.

Protecting our edge analytics applications

Protecting our edge analytics applications may be a simple matter of changing our passwords frequently or placing our edge devices in secure locations. Also, the use of SSL certificates ensures that the data we transmit across the internet is encrypted. In this section, we will discuss some of the methods of ensuring our edge analytics applications are as secure as possible from cyber crime. We will start by looking at passwords.

Passwords and updates

In `Chapter 6`, *Using MicroPython for Edge Analytics*, we used a few microcontrollers as edge devices. Microcontrollers, such as Pycom's LoPy, use default usernames and passwords for both the WiFi access point and FTP file transfers. Not changing these parameters poses a significant security risk when these devices are put in production. To improve security, passwords should be changed from their default settings. It is also good practice to change passwords periodically. Passwords with a mixture of upper- and lowercase letters, numbers, and symbols are stronger than ones without that mixture. Password attacks that use common passwords would have a harder time breaking through devices with stronger and more cryptic passwords. Devices that have hardcoded usernames and passwords should not be used in a production environment.

Cross-site scripting and phishing attack prevention

We should also be aware of attempts to change the passwords of any internet-accessed dashboard we may use. For example, you may receive an email stating that your account has been compromised and a new password is required. Be wary of messages like this and be sure to check the URL on any link provided. Attacks such as this are known as **phishing attacks**. The URL may contain code that records what you type. So, for instance, if you were to click on a link with **cross-site** code, you would be taken to a legitimate website; however, your keystrokes will be recorded.

The following diagram explains this concept graphically:

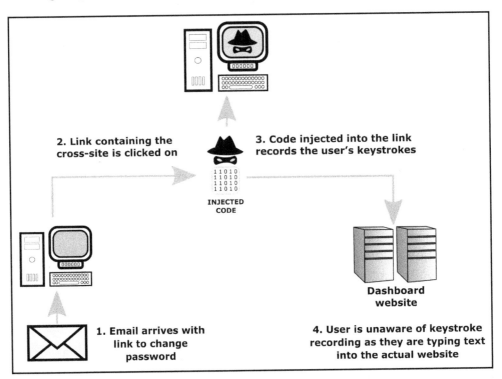

Be wary of emails that provide links to update your account settings. If you are the owner of the website in question, you may take steps to strip away any cross-site scripting code. At the same time, sending a warning to users to not click on links from emails would be a good idea.

Updates to our devices, especially internet routers, are required from time to time. Be sure to schedule a time for doing this and stay away from using default passwords.

Physical security

Often, edge analytics applications are set up in remote locations. Security for applications like this may come down to physically securing hardware in cases that are locked with a key. One option may be to use a key switch attached to a **general-purpose input/output** (**GPIO**) port, where in order to add or change the code on the edge device, a physical key is required to set a flag. An example key switch is shown in the following photo:

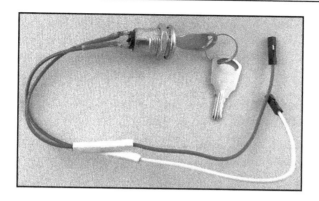

Other options may be to have the edge device shut down if a certain number of unsuccessful login attempts are made.

Using SSL certificates

A simple way to improve the security of our edge analytics applications is to use the SSL port when communicating with an MQTT server. The following is a diagram of an SSL connection:

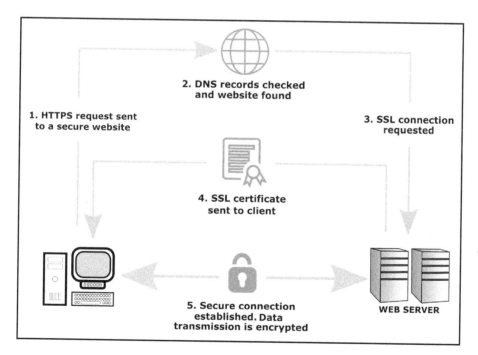

As we can see, when a client requests a connection to a secure website (using `https` in the URL), a certificate is sent to the client once the DNS records are checked and the request made. It is through this certificate that a secure connection is made and established with the client and the secure website.

In order to use SSL for our smart doorbell application, we need to use the SSL port displayed on the **Instance info** page in CloudMQTT, as shown:

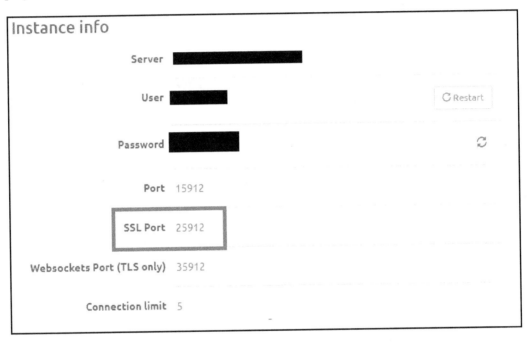

The drawback to using SSL is the extra work that is carried out between the client and the secure website in the form of handshakes and encrypting and decrypting messages. This leads to a performance hit as the extra steps require more time.

Azure Security Center for IoT

Edge analytics applications that use Azure can use Azure Security Center for IoT. The following is a diagram of its architecture:

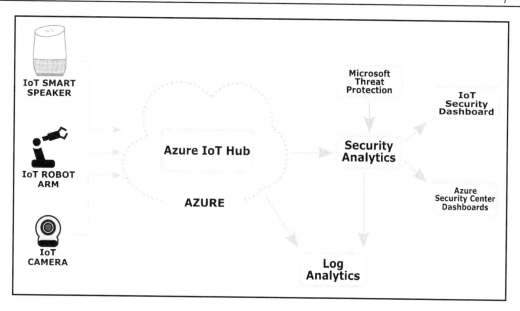

Using the SDK security message, Azure IoT devices send security information to IoT Hub. IoT Hub then forwards this information to analytics modules before passing it along to the Azure Security Center and IoT Security dashboards. Threat intelligence is sent to the IoT Security and Azure Security Center dashboards through the use of the security analytics module.

From the Azure Security Center and IoT Security dashboards, the user can view the security of all their cloud and on-premises workloads, including IoT solutions in Azure, in a unified format. With these services, the user can manage the security policies of their Edge devices and IoT Hub.

With Microsoft Threat Protection and security analytics, the user has an edge over cyber attacks through the use of Microsoft-developed machine learning algorithms that identify the attack. Microsoft invests heavily in threat-protection intelligence in order to offer its customers peace of mind about the security of their Azure deployments.

Monitoring and auditing our edge analytics applications

Security is a big concern for our applications and must be taken into account when building and deploying them. The question we should ask is how do we get on top of it? The key to mitigating security concerns is monitoring and auditing the devices on our applications. By analyzing the traffic that flows into our applications, we can set up alerts to let us know whether there are any possible security threats. Also, by keeping an audit of our devices and addressing possible security concerns before deployment, we can patch known security holes before they become a problem.

Let's take a look at monitoring, first.

Monitoring our edge analytics applications

For edge applications built on the Azure platform, there are various tools and dashboards on Azure Security Center for IoT that can be deployed to monitor security threats. These tools can scan for vulnerabilities in the devices connected to the edge device and make recommendations to the architect about limiting access to certain functions. Tools such as Microsoft Threat Protection can detect suspicious login activity and create alerts of this activity. This is one of the advantages of choosing a big-name provider such as Microsoft when building your edge analytics application.

For edge analytics applications built with standard components, a machine-language module can be built to intercept traffic. The following is a diagram of an example architecture:

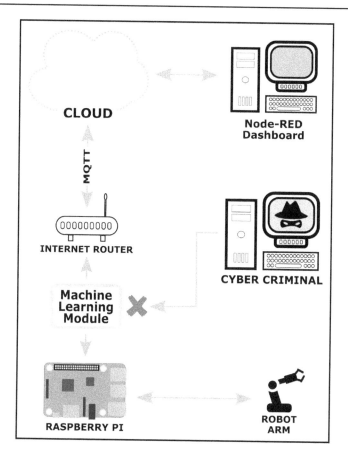

As you can see, requests made to our edge device go through a machine learning module that is designed to look for requests that seem suspicious. These suspicious requests trigger an alarm, indicating that there has been a possible security breach that should be investigated. A module like this could be built using libraries such as TensorFlow, PyTorch, or Keras.

Taking an audit of our edge analytics devices

IoT applications and edge analytics applications are made up of devices with varying operating systems and firmware. You will, most likely, encounter situations where there are varying update schedules for the devices that make up your applications. The following is a list of some actions that can be followed to ensure the smooth auditing of these devices:

- Validate the existence of all the devices that are used in the edge analytics applications in the form of regular inventory counts. This could mean inventory counts for devices that are deployed and devices that are idle.
- Ensure that documentation exists for each device used in the edge analytics application and that the documentation is up to date.
- Verify that architecture diagrams exist and are up to date for the edge analytics applications.
- Ensure that log files are generated for devices that produce them and that the log repository is cleared out to avoid storage issues.
- Ensure that configuration files are present and up to date for the devices that require them.
- Verify that each device has the latest software or firmware patches (updates may lag behind the update cycles from the manufacturers due to patch-testing requirements).
- Ensure that the response plans for the event of an application failure are up to date and understood by those working with the application.

Summary

In this chapter, we started our discussion on security and privacy by describing a cyber attack involving IoT devices. Although our edge analytics applications offer a bit of a buffer against the unauthorized use of devices, there is still a lot that should concern us when it comes to security.

We then looked at some of the various types of attacks that we should look out for when building and deploying our applications. These include issues with vulnerability, sniffing of our data, and spoofing of our devices, such that our application confuses the fake device for one of our own.

We then took a look at how we can protect our edge analytics applications by confirming the updates of passwords and security patches. We discussed how physical security can be implemented to keep remote devices safe. We also looked at how secure internet connections work and took a high-level look at Azure Security Center for IoT.

In the final chapter, we will take a glimpse into what the future may hold for edge analytics.

Questions

Having read this chapter, try answering the following questions on your own:

1. True/False. The code used in the Mirai botnet attack in 2016 was released to the public in order to create plausible deniability for the creators.
2. True/False. A command and control server is used in DDoS attacks.
3. What is a cross-site scripting attack?
4. Name three of the possible types of attacks against our edge analytics applications.
5. True/False. A sniffer is a type of spying tool that is set up between our internet router and edge computer.
6. How does a cyber criminal trick you into giving them your username and password when you log on to a legitimate website?
7. True/False. A physical key switch can be used as a form of security protection on our edge device.
8. What are some of the libraries that we can use to write a machine learning module?
9. True/False. The name of the Microsoft tool used to monitor security threats is called Azure Security Center for IoT.
10. True/False. Ensuring that device configuration files are up to date is good practice when taking an audit of the devices used on our applications.

Further reading

For more information about Azure Security Center for IoT, go to `https://docs.microsoft.com/en-us/azure/asc-for-iot/overview`.

10
What Next?

As I write these words, the entire world is in a state of lockdown due to the COVID-19 pandemic. Extraordinary times, to say the least. However bleak the situation may be—and at this point, there is much to feel anxious about—it is at times such as these where humanity's ingenuity rises to the occasion. Many in the maker community, which I am a part of, have with astonishing speed taken to creating **personal protective equipment (PPE)** with 3D printers for those on the front lines. Factories designed to produce cars have quickly transitioned to making much-needed medical equipment. Entertainers continue to entertain us, teachers continue to teach their students, and leaders continue to inform us, all through the miracle of modern video and internet technologies.

Somewhere, the next Isaac Newton is using the time in lockdown developing the next breakthrough technology or world-changing formula, just as Newton himself did waiting out the Great Plague of the mid-1660s. Hopefully, by the time you read these words, the worst is behind us and a new future is opening up—one where technology will continue to lead the way to a better life.

In this book, we've covered the *how* in edge analytics. It's now time to look back at what we've learned and use it to predict the future—a better future: the reason why we spend our time learning new technologies.

In this chapter, we will cover the following topics:

- Recapping what we have learned about edge analytics
- Looking at the future of edge analytics

Recapping what we have learned about edge analytics

We covered a lot of ground in this book, from exploring what edge analytics is, to creating a smart doorbell that announces our visitors. Let's review what we learned in each chapter.

Chapter 1

In this chapter, we compared the distributed computing nature of an edge analytics application to distributed computing brought about by the introduction of the personal computer, distributed computing being a move away from a central mainframe computer. Although far from being a perfect analogy, this comparison drove home the point that information technology does seem to go back and forth from centralized processing to distributed processing.

We described ways in which a standard **Internet of Things** (**IoT**) solution differs from an edge analytics one in the way sensory information is processed on the *edge*. We compared an IoT approach in a fictional vending-machine business with an edge analytics one and discussed the benefits of the latter.

We also started looking at the three key benefits of edge analytics—*privacy*, *latency*, and *reliability*. We further divided our research into edge analytics by looking at basic edge analytics architectures and compared them to vendor-specific architectures. Basic architectures allowed us the freedom to choose our edge device, while the vendor-specific architectures—in this case, Microsoft Azure IoT Edge—gave us the support of a well-entrenched vendor.

Chapter 2

In this chapter, we took a deeper look into how edge analytics works. We looked at some of the sensors we may use to measure the world around us, as well as a few of the devices that may serve as our edge devices. Part of the chapter was devoted to looking at some of the amazing microcontrollers available on the market today. As these microcontrollers become more and more powerful, we will certainly see a day when they will replace computers with operating systems as the brains behind an edge analytics application.

We dug a little deeper into Microsoft Azure IoT Edge, providing a background to be used in future chapters.

In our tutorial, we built a weather predictor using an ESP-12F microcontroller and a **red, green, and blue (RGB) light-emitting diode (LED)**. The weather predictor served as a good example of processing on the *edge*, as logic built into the app looked at barometric pressure changes to determine whether the output should be a green light or a red light.

Chapter 3

In this chapter, we looked at the communication protocols used in edge analytics. We explored the **radio frequency (RF)** spectrum and looked at various applications and where they sat on the spectrum. We also discussed the difference between the analog use and the digital use of the word *bandwidth*.

We took a brief look at Bluetooth, as well as some of the long-range wireless technologies used by IoT and edge analytics applications. A look at the Friis transmission equation allowed us to make a case for lower or higher frequencies, depending on the application.

Chapter 4

In this chapter, we turned our full attention to Microsoft Azure IoT Hub. This involved expanding our knowledge on the use of cloud service providers and what they offer us. We looked at virtual machines, as well as containers and serverless computing. We compared these services to the services that Microsoft Azure offers—**infrastructure as a service (IaaS), platform as a service (PaaS), software as a service (SaaS)**, and **function as a service (FaaS)**.

The tutorial in this chapter gave us our first hands-on experience with Microsoft Azure as we built a simulated temperature sensor using Python and connected it to an Azure IoT Hub. Using the Device Explorer tool from Microsoft, we were able to view the simulated data by connecting to the same Azure IoT Hub.

Chapter 5

In this chapter, we installed Microsoft Azure IoT Edge onto a Raspberry Pi 3 computer. Along the way, we learned about installing older versions of the Raspbian operating system, as well as touching on what Moby is.

Our tutorial involved sending out simulated temperature telemetry data using the `SimulatedTemperatureSensor` module from Azure Marketplace.

Chapter 6

If you got anything out of this chapter, I hope it is an appreciation of just how powerful microcontrollers have become. Chapter 6 was dedicated to microcontrollers and their version of the Python 3 programming language, MicroPython. In this chapter, we learned what MicroPython is and how it compares to Arduino C.

We looked at some of the microcontrollers that MicroPython may be installed on, before trying our hand at installing the language onto an ESP32 microcontroller.

Our tutorial simulated a smart heating system for an ice rink and incorporated the **Long Range (LoRa)** communication protocol for sending messages between microcontrollers.

Chapter 7

In this chapter, we explored machine learning and how it applies to edge analytics. We got hands-on experience with the OpenCV image library, as we used it to determine whether a picture contained a human face.

Using a Maix K210 microcontroller, we wrote a program that deciphers a **Quick Response (QR)** code.

Chapter 8

In this chapter, we reached the pinnacle of hands-on edge analytics as we built a smart doorbell application that recognizes a visitor at the door. Using an object-oriented coding approach, we were able to keep our code neat and efficient.

We utilized an external **Message Queuing Telemetry Transport (MQTT)** server to publish simple messages to our dashboard, thereby driving home the edge analytics benefits of *privacy*, *latency*, and *reliability*, as image processing and recognition are done at the *edge*.

Chapter 9

Security and privacy are of the utmost importance for any application that uses the internet. In this chapter, we looked at the various ways our applications may be hit by a *cyber attack*. We looked at ways of protecting ourselves, as well as taking the time to create a list we may use to audit the devices used in our edge analytics applications.

Looking at the future of edge analytics

When I was a child, an image of a future space station caught my eye. It was an artist's rendition of the inside of a giant spinning doughnut-shaped world where centrifugal force would simulate gravity. There were trees and roads and buildings. People were going about their daily lives. The part of the picture that I noticed the most was the horizon as it faded in the upward direction. As this was a picture from inside the doughnut-shaped space station, this made sense. I pictured myself living on such a space station. That image helped set in motion my lifelong interest in science and technology.

"We wanted flying cars, instead we got 140 characters."

–Peter Thiel

Like Peter Thiel, I thought we would have flying cars and giant rotating space stations by now. We don't. That doesn't mean that the technology of today is any less amazing. What it does mean is that predicting the future is, at best, a guess. The following scenario is my guess at what we may expect from an edge analytics future.

A day in the life of Oliver

The year is 2045. Oliver is late for work. He stayed out too late the night before and despite the constant droning from his alarm clock, he just couldn't wake up.

"Wake up, Oliver," his alarm clock would say repeatedly.

"Just 5 more minutes," an exhausted Oliver would respond.

Oliver is 24 years old. He is part of the New Baby Boom Generation that came into the world shortly after the great virus lockdowns of the early 2020s. Oliver works as a technician at an automated factory, not far from where he lives.

Factories in 2045 are not like the factories of today. For one thing, they exemplify lights-out manufacturing. Everything is automated. Robots do not need light to work, so most of the time the lights are off. Factories are no longer set up just to make one or two products anymore. Every factory is a Flex factory and can make pretty much any product. This allows for a distributed approach to manufacturing and supply chain management.

No longer does a product have to be produced months in advance and put on a big container ship, to travel thousands of kilometers just to reach its market. No longer are there lags in supply and demand that often result in a glut of unwanted inventory. Products are produced at almost the same time as they are needed and in a location close to the customer. Products may also be customized on demand. This zero-inventory and mass-product customization model reduces waste and improves customer satisfaction. Each factory is connected to every other factory but maintains its autonomy through the use of edge analytics. The following diagram shows such a factory:

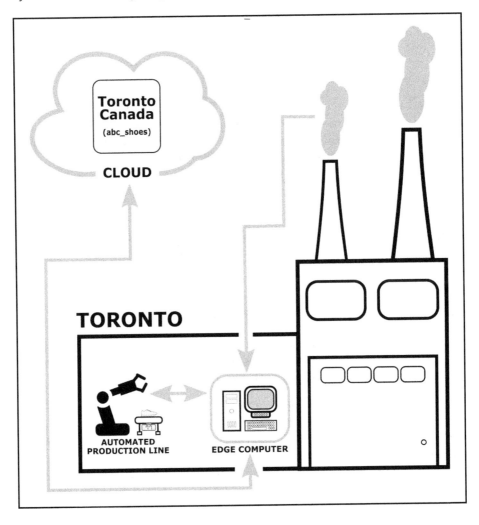

Oliver works at the TORONTO factory, so named for its proximity to the metropolis that is Toronto, Canada. The population of Toronto has grown exponentially in the last couple of decades, so much so that the TORONTO factory is running 24 hours a day at full capacity.

In each automated factory such as the TORONTO factory lies a super-powerful edge computer. This edge computer handles communications coming from the cloud, such as orders and remote dashboard requests. It also monitors the pollution level emitted and turns on the pollution scrubbers so that only clean, breathable air leaves the smokestacks of the factory. In addition, the edge supercomputer communicates with the edge computers used in the automated production line.

On this particular day, orders for the latest shoes, *ABC shoes*, are coming into the factory. The marketing blitz was spectacularly successful, and automated factories throughout the world are working non-stop to produce the shoes.

Oliver spends his working day monitoring the online dashboards, which are generated by communication with the factory edge computer. It can be pretty boring, as everything runs smoothly the vast majority of the time and there is not a lot to do. Outside of the monthly on-site meetings with the other technicians, he is pretty much free to work remotely, communicating with his team through video chat.

He is late logging in and doesn't have time to groom himself properly. He knows he is going to be teased by his co-workers, so he just puts on a baseball cap and hopes that no one notices his lateness. He can barely keep awake as he scans his fingerprint to log in to his computer. Most of the time, he can slip into the dashboard system a little late without anyone making a fuss. However, this morning is different from other mornings. One alarm after another flashes on his screen. He joins the video conference midway and tries to catch up with the conversation that is already in progress.

"Nice of you to join us, Oliver!" splashes across the bottom of his screen. Oliver is awake now.

Production is falling behind schedule. A machine in section H7 has stopped.

A big drawback to inventoryless business models is the pressure it puts on production lines. Even a few minutes of delay can cost a company a lot of money. Oliver requests to take the lead and share his screen with the others, in an attempt to have his lateness immediately forgotten. He is granted permission.

He is able to remotely control a factory floor robot and display what the robot sees on his screen. He guides the robot to the problem area, as indicated by the dashboard alarms. Using the robot's infrared vision, he spots an issue with a power cord. Zooming in, he can see that the cord has been damaged. He guides the robot toward the cord to get a closer look. Theories as to the cause of the damage flash across the chat panel of the screen as the robot gets closer.

"RODENTS!" yells Oliver.

By now, Oliver is feeling pretty good about himself. He's wide awake and his lateness is now ancient history.

"OK," says one co-worker. *"Someone has to go in and fix it."*

"Where is everyone today?" asks another.

A map pops up on everyone's screen, showing the locations of all the participants on the video conference. Some of the participants look like they've really taken the remote thing seriously, and are located in parts of the world with much better climates than Toronto, Canada. Oliver doesn't feel so bad about being late once in a while.

"OK, who can get there the fastest?" asks one of the participants.

Another map pops up with driving directions and commuting times to the TORONTO factory for each of the video-conference participants. It would take a stopover flight in Chicago and a 2-hour Uber ride for Archie to get there. So, he's unavailable.

"Looks like you're the one, Oliver," says a chorus of relieved co-workers.

Oliver wasn't planning on commuting today. Sitting in his self-driving car for an hour isn't his idea of a good time, but this time, he gladly steps up to the task. At least he can catch up on some online training he has been putting off.

In 2045, self-driving cars are finally a reality. Many a political battle was waged before self-driving cars were accepted as the better option for increasingly crowded streets and highways. The following diagram shows a self-driving car network in 2045:

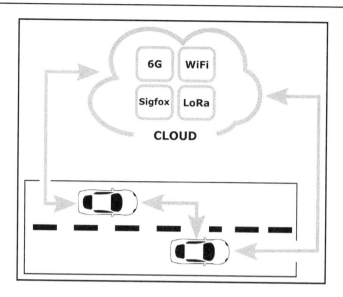

Each self-driving car contains an edge computer that reads sensory information such as the white and yellow highway lines and the location of other cars and objects around the car. The car's edge computer also communicates directly with other self-driving cars. The car can send geolocation and diagnostic data to the cloud and receive updates on road conditions and travel times. 6G is the preferred communication protocol when it is available. Wi-Fi is used when the car is parked at home or at the office. LoRa and Sigfox are used in more remote areas. Even though LoRa is now available throughout the entire world due to LoRa communication satellite launches in the 2030s, it is still used sparingly due to its limited bandwidth.

Oliver is a little hungry, so he grabs an energy food bar and heads to his garage. As he unplugs the car from its charging port, the lights inside the car turn on and the doors are unlocked. His video session is automatically transferred to the main screen in the car.

"If you don't mind, guys, I have some training to catch up on," Oliver says, as he minimizes the video-conference window on the screen.

"Go ahead," says the co-worker logged in from a cottage in the Florida Keys.

"Take me to TORONTO," Oliver says to the edge computer in the car.

"Right away," responds the edge computer.

"You should arrive at the TORONTO factory in 55 minutes and 29 seconds," adds the edge computer.

Oliver calls up the training video he's been putting off. After a few minutes, he can barely keep his eyes open. The video is so boring. Oliver falls asleep as his self-driving car heads toward the factory.

As Oliver sleeps, conversations are still going on in the video conference. An hour is a long time to respond to a production-line shutdown. Many start to worry about what the future will hold. When TORONTO first opened, there was always someone on site. Gradually, the factory was automated to the point where technicians merely needed to monitor the systems and could guide robots to fix any issues that would arise. No one could remember the last time a robot couldn't fix something.

Oliver is woken up by the car's edge computer.

"You have arrived, Oliver," says the car.

Oliver does not see a single person as he opens the car door. During on-site meetings, there are usually many people around. It is an eerie sight. Oliver walks up to the main doors. Keys are not needed as face and voice recognition are used to gain access to the factory. Oliver takes off his baseball cap and looks into the camera.

"Hi, it's Oliver. I'm here to investigate an issue in section H7," he says.

Within seconds, Oliver is identified as a valid visitor, and the automated door opens. The following diagram shows an automated door system:

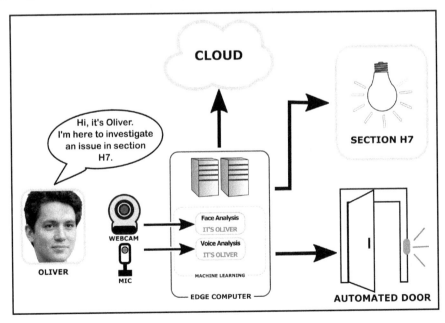

The machine learning algorithms that recognize Oliver also recognize the path Oliver should take to get to section H7. The walkways leading to H7 are lit up, guiding Oliver to the affected area. The online factory dashboard is updated, informing Oliver's co-workers of his arrival at the factory. His co-workers are relieved.

Oliver finds the faulty plug, and within a few minutes is able to change it for a new one. The production line in section H7 starts up again. Oliver documents his work on the company database, using his phone. He makes a note of the difficulty the current factory-floor robots have with changing cords and suggests an upgrade. He also recommends bringing in an exterminator to deal with the rodents. His notes will be brought up at the next on-site meeting.

The factory edge computer illuminates Oliver's path out of the factory. He jumps in his self-driving car and heads home.

Oliver goes to bed early that night.

What will your future be like?

It is usually at this point in a chapter that I present you with questions to test your knowledge of the subjects covered. Class is dismissed early this time and there will be no quiz. Instead, I would like you to think of your future and how you may take what we've covered in this book and turn it into something awesome.

Thank you for joining me on this journey.

Other Books You May Enjoy

If you enjoyed this book, you may be interested in these other books by Packt:

IoT and Edge Computing for Architects - Second Edition
Perry Lea

ISBN: 978-1-83921-480-6

- Understand the role and scope of architecting a successful IoT deployment
- Scan the landscape of IoT technologies, from sensors to the cloud and more
- See the trade-offs in choices of protocols and communications in IoT deployments
- Become familiar with the terminology needed to work in the IoT space
- Broaden your skills in the multiple engineering domains necessary for the IoT architect
- Implement best practices to ensure reliability, scalability, and security in your IoT infrastructure

Mastering Azure Machine Learning

Christoph Körner, Kaijisse Waaijer

ISBN: 978-1-78980-755-4

- Setup your Azure ML workspace for data experimentation and visualization
- Perform ETL, data preparation, and feature extraction using Azure best practices
- Implement advanced feature extraction using NLP and word embeddings
- Train gradient boosted tree-ensembles, recommendation engines and deep neural networks on Azure ML
- Use hyperparameter tuning and AutoML to optimize your ML models
- Employ distributed ML on GPU clusters using Horovod in Azure ML
- Deploy, operate and manage your ML models at scale
- Automated your end-to-end ML process as CI/CD pipelines for MLOps

Leave a review - let other readers know what you think

Please share your thoughts on this book with others by leaving a review on the site that you bought it from. If you purchased the book from Amazon, please leave us an honest review on this book's Amazon page. This is vital so that other potential readers can see and use your unbiased opinion to make purchasing decisions, we can understand what our customers think about our products, and our authors can see your feedback on the title that they have worked with Packt to create. It will only take a few minutes of your time, but is valuable to other potential customers, our authors, and Packt. Thank you!

Index

CPSIA information can be obtained
at www.ICGtesting.com
Printed in the USA
LVHW101545070620
657619LV00007B/302